ADVANCE PRAISE FOR

UBUNTU PEDAGOGY: BECOMING AN UBUNTU-RESPONSIVE EDUCATOR

"We are in a time when educational leaders and teachers are rethinking what we teach, how we teach it and how to provide effective social emotional support to students. Through *Ubuntu Pedagogy*, Dr. Alecia Blackwood provides a culturally rich, relevant and responsive framework for centering students humanity in the classroom, leading to authentic engagement and achievement."

Chike Akua, PhD
Associate Professor of Educational Leadership
Clark Atlanta University
Author: Education for Transformation:
The Keys to Releasing the Genius of African American Students

"We are presented with an excellent pedagogy where education evolves from being an abstract experience into a creative and adaptive practice. The author skillfully uses Ubuntu storytelling and a performative approach to illustrate how to become an Ubuntu-Responsive educator. A must read for educators invested in cultivating an inclusive classroom environment rooted in a transformative learning culture."

Michael Onyebuchi Eze
Africana Studies, California State University, Fresno

"To have Ubuntu is to be a person who is living a genuinely human way of life and exhibits its human excellence. Dr. Alecia Blackwood embodies Ubuntu not only in her teaching, but also in her very being. Her teaching exposes educators to how Ubuntu ways can enhance their teaching and exhilarate their students. But, Dr.Alecia Blackwood has a deeper purpose to her teaching: she embodies and models the human excellence so that teachers and students learn Ubuntu ways in practice and in life. This 2nd edition of *Ubuntu Pedagogy: Becoming an Ubuntu-Responsive Educator* continues her excellent work to impact educators nationally and internationally."

Carolyn Walker Hopp, PhD
Retired Faculty
College of Community Innovation and Education
University of Central Florida

"In *Ubuntu Pedagogy: Becoming an Ubuntu-Responsive Educator*, Dr. Alecia Blackwood- an esteemed educator, author, and editor- presents a rich second edition. Drawing from her extensive experiences, she examines the evolving role of Ubuntu in education. She invites us to consider traditional African philosophy, practice, and teaching methods to assess teaching and learning. This book is essential for educators and embracing a racial cultural perspective and ways to create learning environments."

Hassiem Ayele Kambui, PhD
Professor of Counseling, College of Education
Florida Agricultural and Mechanical University (FAMU)

UBUNTU PEDAGOGY

UBUNTU PEDAGOGY

Becoming an Ubuntu-Responsive Educator

BY ALECIA BLACKWOOD

Myers Education Press

Gorham, Maine

Published by Myers Education Press, LLC
P.O. Box 424
Gorham, ME 04038

Myers Education Press is an academic publisher specializing in books, e-books and digital content in the field of education. All of our books are subjected to a rigorous peer review process and produced in compliance with the standards of the Council on Library and Information Resources.

Library of Congress Cataloging-in-Publication Data available from Library of Congress.

13-digit ISBN 978-1-9755-0749-7 (paperback)
13-digit ISBN 978-1-9755-0750-3 (library networkable e-edition)
13-digit ISBN 978-1-9755-0751-0 (consumer e-edition)

Printed in the United States of America.

All first editions printed on acid-free paper that meets the American National Standards Institute Z39-48 standard.

Cover design by Teresa Lagrange

Contents

Acknowledgments

I want to thank Dr. Ominutuo Ukpokodu, the seminal writer on Ubuntu pedagogy who worked hard to promote the concept of Ubuntu in academia.

I AM GIVING HONOR TO THE divine creator for allowing me to be the vehicle to share this experience with the world. To all my ancestors, Grandma Myrtle Josephs, Rupert Mclean, and Nana Baba Fritz Lewis, thank you for instilling the value of education in me. I appreciate the support of all my elders who have guided me on this journey. Also, my profound thanks to my birth mother, Petrona Mclean, for all your sacrifices to make sure I had an education.

Many thanks to my beloved *Jegnoch* (master teachers), Dr. Carolyn Walker-Hopp, and Olabesi Olakolade, for your unwavering support and encouragement. To Dr. Kevin Mwata Washington, who introduced me to the concept of Ubuntu, I thank you because your words turned the light on in my eyes and changed the trajectory of my life!

Thanks to all my family members, especially Nigel, Shebana, Prince, and Aunt Judy, who encouraged me. To my sacred sister circle, Empress Power, much love for support and words of encouragement. To the staff and children at Afrikan Kulcha School and Nap Ford Community School, where I have grown and honed my craft as a teacher for over 20 years, thank you for helping me become an Ubuntu-responsive educator.

To all my colleagues and the teachers who send positive vibes and encouragement to continue authoring this book, I am grateful for that energy that pushes me forward. I am most thankful for Queen Taese, who always validated my work and encouraged me to write the book.

Thanks for being my biggest cheerleader—Dr. Hassiem Ayele Kambui. Your weekly check-ins on the book's progress have encouraged and kept me writing. I remember every time I picked up the phone, you would say, "Hey Doc, how is the book? What did you work on?" Thank you for being a fantastic accountability partner. Your words have motivated me to complete this project. To my serial author, friend, and publisher, Ankwetta Beatrice Achaleke, thank you for inspiring and coaching me through this writing process and providing words of wisdom and inspiration. The writers' affirmations you sent helped me overcome my obstacles.

To all my womb children and community children, Tsahaywattak, Mirrikattiwat, Selamdesta, Mabrak, Inefta, Tesfayealem, a Hailee, and Djahnya, who have been in my classroom, thank you for your feedback. Also, to all the parents who have said to me, "you are a good teacher," those words have helped inspire this book. Special thanks to the many elders, teachers, friends, and students who have supported and influenced me significantly. I cannot name you all here but know that I am grateful for the dialogue, feedback, questions, and support.

Additionally, I honor all my historical *Ankhcestors*[1] (ancestors), Marva Collins, Dr. Amos Wilson, and Dr. Asa G. Hillard III, for the wisdom they shared with me via speeches or books. *Ase*!

[1] An Ankhcestor is an ancestor who has significantly contributed to life that will benefit generations.

Preface

IN A WORLD INCREASINGLY SHAPED by diverse cultures and interconnected communities, the principle of Ubuntu stands out as a profound philosophy gifted to the world by Africa. Ubuntu emphasizes human interdependence, compassion, and collective solidarity. Although this concept is not new, it has been popularized in the Western world by leaders such as former U.S. Presidents Bill Clinton and Barack Obama. African leaders like President Nelson Mandela and Archbishop Desmond Tutu have also elaborated on Ubuntu during their engagements in the West.

Ubuntu has permeated various sectors globally, including business leadership, the tech world, and education. At its core, Ubuntu speaks to the essence of our humanity. In my classroom, I use it to center students' humanity. Ubuntu's philosophy has profoundly impacted my teaching style. In education, I refer to this approach as "Ubuntu pedagogy," a humanistic approach to teaching and learning that prioritizes human-centric values.

This book, *Ubuntu Pedagogy: Becoming an Ubuntu-Responsive Educator*, seeks to illuminate the transformative potential of Ubuntu in educational settings. The journey to writing this book began with my lived experiences and how cultivating a sense of community in my classroom transformed my approach to teaching and learning. I started this journey with the foundational knowledge of culturally relevant teaching proposed by Gloria Ladson-Billings and a deep-seated belief in every individual's inherent worth and dignity, as espoused by Geneva Gay's culturally responsive teaching. From this solid foundation, I cultivated a culture of love and care, revolutionizing how I teach students. Throughout my teaching, I prioritize students' inherent dignity, affirming and validating every learner.

As an educator with over 25 years of experience, I have witnessed firsthand the profound impact of culturally responsive teaching. Through deep self-study, I was able to pinpoint what it sounds and looks like in the classroom as teachers grow from mere awareness to critical consciousness. My quest to understand what it means "to teach in the spirit of Ubuntu" led me to discover more about myself as an educator and how to support and build the confidence of every learner in my learning spaces. Learning about the philosophy of Ubuntu has helped to reawaken the gifts in every child and foster a more inclusive, compassionate, and equitable learning environment where every child succeeds.

Ubuntu pedagogy is more than an instructional method; it is a way of being that acknowledges our shared humanity and interconnectedness. It calls upon educators to view their students not merely as recipients of knowledge but as co-creators in the learning process. Ubuntu pedagogy is a perfect antidote to counteract what Paulo Freire calls the "banking concept" and any other form of colonizing pedagogy that dehumanizes the learner. Ubuntu pedagogy rejects the banking concept, in which the teacher is the sole narrator depositing knowledge into passive student receptacles. Instead, it views the learner-teacher relationship as a partnership of co-creators, nurturing democratic classroom environments where students' voices, experiences, and cultural identities are affirmed as assets to build knowledge collectively. This approach nurtures a classroom atmosphere where respect, care, and mutual growth are paramount, challenging the hierarchical structures that often define traditional education. Ubuntu pedagogy empowers students to critically analyze dominant narratives of society, cultivate critical consciousness, and develop counter-narratives rooted in their own cultural epistemologies. Furthermore, Ubuntu pedagogy is grounded in a humanizing approach that affirms both students and teachers. It fosters nurturing relationships, cooperative learning, affirmation of cultural identities, and the development of critical consciousness. In writing this book, I draw upon a wealth of personal experiences, scholarly research, and practical examples to provide a comprehensive guide for educators. The chapters ahead explore the philosophical foundations of Ubuntu, the dynamics of learner-teacher relationships, and the practical applications of Ubuntu principles in the classroom.

Ubuntu pedagogy offers a worldview different from that of traditional pedagogy. Ubuntu pedagogy views the learner-teacher relationship as a partnership of co-creators of knowledge, promoting mutual respect, care, and affirmation of humanity. Traditional pedagogy incorporates more Western individualistic and Eurocentric worldviews with a more hierarchical power dynamic in the classroom. Students from collectivist cultures learn best when they feel a sense of connection and belonging. The Ubuntu pedagogy framework guides teachers on how to be a reflective educator and create learning spaces where students feel validated and dignified as human beings. Unlike traditional pedagogies that approach teaching from an authoritarian standpoint, Ubuntu pedagogy encourages educators to create learning spaces that nurture democratic classroom environments where students feel respected, cared for, and free to co-learn.

Meanwhile, traditional pedagogies focus more on individualism and competition. Ubuntu pedagogy emphasizes cooperative learning, drawing on diverse perspectives and experiences to build knowledge collectively. Ubuntu pedagogy also affirms students' cultural identities and Indigenous knowledge as assets upon which to build. Students' cultures are affirmed so they don't feel marginalized, as they do in classrooms that use Students' cultures are affirmed to prevent feelings of marginalization, unlike in classrooms that rely on traditional Western pedagogy frameworks. The purpose of this book is to help educators cultivate a mindset that promotes love, joy, cooperation, and human dignity alongside academic learning. Traditional teaching style primarily focuses on academic content mastery. Ubuntu pedagogy's main goal is to center the humanity of the learner before teaching the content. Ubuntu pedagogy seeks to restore all students' cultural identities and decolonize the education systems. See the chart in Appendix D.

Each chapter of the book offers insights and strategies to help educators create learning environments that honor all students' cultural identities and experiences. My hope is that the book also helps further enhance a deep understanding of critical consciousness in teaching. I'll guide you through what it sounds and looks like and the specific pedagogical actions involved. We anchor these insights within the six components of Ubuntu pedagogy, transcending basic knowledge of culturally responsive teaching to foster a transformative shift toward Ubuntu competence. *Ubuntu Pedagogy: Becoming an Ubuntu-Responsive Educator* is both a call to action and a resource for educators committed to fostering a more humane and just educational system. It invites you to embark on a journey of personal and professional growth, embracing Ubuntu as a teaching philosophy and a way of life. May this book inspire you to cultivate classrooms where every student feels valued, respected, and empowered to contribute to the collective well-being of our evolving global community. As you turn these pages, I hope you find the inspiration and practical tools to become an Ubuntu-responsive educator, championing a pedagogy that is as transformative as it is compassionate.

Book Overview

THIS BOOK WAS BORN OUT of my lived experience teaching in schools in the United States of America. The purpose of the book is to provide a narrative of my experience and how I used the concept of Ubuntu in my teaching practices to engage the learners actively. In the book, I explore what it means to teach in the spirit of Ubuntu and provide practical examples of pedagogical moves that I used to engage with all learners actively.

Furthermore, I provide a conceptual framework of Ubuntu pedagogy and show how teaching in a humanistic way benefits all learners. The book also captures how the knowledge and practices of Ubuntu pedagogy transform my teaching practices and improve students' overall achievement.

Introduction

The introduction provides a historical context of the people and culture of Southern Africa, mainly the Zulu worldview that gave birth to the ancient concept of Ubuntu. In this book, readers will learn about the author's journey from the Americas to Southern Africa, the land of the Bantu people, which teaches us about the essence of Ubuntu.

Part One

This part captures the author's story as she reflects on her tumultuous experience as a first-year teacher in a large urban public school district. The author reflects on the traumatic experience of 9/11 and how that impacted her teaching in the early 2000s. Also, the author shows how and why it is crucial to engage in reflective practices as an educator.

Part Two

This part captures what it means to teach in the spirit of Ubuntu. In this section, the author outlines and explains the six components of teaching in the spirit of Ubuntu. Understanding self and how to build positive relationships with self and others are critical elements of Ubuntu-oriented style of teaching. Additionally, the author explains how and why it is essential to create unity among students and teach from a position of love and care. Finally, the author explores how to use evidence-based practices to meet the diverse needs of all learners.

Part Three

This part is about the author's experiences working with children and teachers in rural and inner-city schools in Botswana and Namibia. The author details her experiences and observations she made when she lived and worked in southern Africa. As an outsider, the author talks about the evidence of how Ubuntu was being demonstrated in the schools.

Part Four

This part examines Ubuntu and discipline and how the idea of an Ubuntu discipline approach plays a role in creating a harmonious learning environment where students can grow and learn.

Part Five

Part Five is about the critical characteristics of cultural competence versus Ubuntu competence. The author explains what it means to be a competent teacher. The big focus is on teachers in the field sharing their experiences working in inner-city schools in the United States of America.

Part Six

Part Six explores who we are as teachers and how we teach who we are in the classroom. Furthermore, the author provides step-by-step guidance on creating our teaching philosophy.

Part Seven

Part Seven discusses Ubuntu in action, focusing on how to cultivate good character among students. The author also provides practical applications of proverbs, aphorisms, and adinkra symbols to develop good character and help students make good choices.

Why Is Ubuntu Pedagogy So Necessary for the 21st Century?

Message from
Dr. Omiunota N. Ukpokodu, PhD

PAULO FREIRE (1978) WRITES THAT education can act as an instrument of humanization and dehumanization and asks that we choose the former. As a student of Freire, a multicultural and transformative educator and scholar for decades, I couldn't agree more!

Today's world is more characteristically, dramatically, and demographically different than ever. It is culturally diverse, intricately interdependent, and interconnected. Students of the 21st century and beyond need new and complex knowledge, skills, attitudes, and values to live and participate in it. Precisely, they must possess a critical cultural competence to live their full humanity and exemplify the cardinal principle of "I in you and you in me" or "I am because we are and because we are therefore, I am" in their individual and collective life. More importantly, they must possess critical consciousness to analyze social realities, gain perspective consciousness, make meaning, and act to disrupt systemic inequities, injustice, and dehumanization. Students can only cultivate these complex skills and competencies in learning spaces that are humane and dialogical and with educators who value and affirm their humanity and dignity.

For students who have been "otherized," marginalized, disenfranchised, and disconnected, Ubuntu pedagogy accords them the opportunity to actively engage, learn, grow, and academically thrive in a community of respect, love, humility, care, and responsibility. Ubuntu pedagogy emboldens educators to unleash their humanity, transcend the traditional, be organic, and be empowered to engage their practice with love, hope, possibility, compassionate intellectualism, and change agency.

Ubuntu pedagogy is not only necessary but is nonnegotiable for 21st-century classrooms. It is transformative and the perfect antidote to the pervasive, oppressive, and "colonizing" pedagogy used across many schools. Ubuntu pedagogy accords and restores students' humanity in the practice of education for freedom. Because it honors and affirms students' humanity, it values and utilizes their "funds of knowledge," making their learning culturally responsive, empowering, and relevant (O. Ukpokodu, personal communication, July 3, 2017).

References

Freire, P. (1978). *Pedagogy of the oppressed*. Continuum.

Introduction

South Africa (Azania), Ubuntu, and Zulu Cosmology

By Kevin Mwata Washington, PhD

Brief Overview of South Africa

The Republic of South Africa was created in 1910. It is located at the southernmost tip of the African continent. It is comprised of San (Bushmen), Nguni people (Xhosa, Zulu, Swati, Ndebele), Sotho (Tswana, Sesotho, and Sepedi), Tsonga people, Venda people, Coloureds, Indians, Afrikaners, and English. The country is divided into nine provinces: the Western Cape, the Eastern Cape, the Northern Cape, the Free State, the Kwa-Zulu Natal, the Northwest, Gauteng, Mpumalanga, and the Northern Province. These provinces are a recent development; however, this world region has a long history. The world owes to South Africa the promotion and revitalization of the concept of Ubuntu. Ubuntu is a Nguni word from the Bantu people.

The earliest recorded inhabitants of what is now called South Africa were the San. Researchers estimate that the San extended 100,000 years ago. The Khoikhoi seems to have appeared later. Their history is approximately 2,000 years old. Approximately 1,000 years ago, immigrant Bantu speakers began to work in the land, mainly in the river valleys of southeastern Africa. In the 1600s, Europeans began to colonize the land. First the Portuguese and later the Dutch, English, and French moved in because they all saw the Cape as a strategic route to the East. They were able to provide a rest stop for their trading ships traveling to and from the East by establishing posts in the southern tip of Africa. The Dutch set up a mainland base in 1652. Their settlement greatly concerned the *Khoikhoi*, and they established a base to provide food, water, and other maritime needs. It became apparent to the *Khoikhoi* that the Dutch did not seek peaceful coexistence. Therefore, the *Khoikhoi* began to resist working with (for) the Dutch. The opportunistic Dutch desired cheap (free) labor and were willing to do anything to realize their desires. Not only did they strive to collaborate with the inhabitants of South Africa, but they also brought enslaved Africans from other parts of Africa to the region for labor and pleasure.

Early on, the enslaved Africans resisted enslavement and the evil encroachment of the Dutch with some success. The riotous group of Europeans moved into present-day South Africa (Azania), looting, raping, stealing, deceiving, pillaging, killing, and manipulating. Years of battles with Europeans' raucous culture took a significant toll on Indigenous African populations. By the 1880s, the San had been forced from their original settlement across the Orange (Gariep) River. The Dutch continued to be a rowdy and violent bunch and went to war with all Indigenous Africans.

In addition to wanting more power, they dominated the Africans; they wanted to acquire the land for their benefit. They were unwilling to share the land as the original inhabitants were willing to do. After disrupting the life of the San, the Bantu and Khoikhoi encountered the European intruders in the conflict between the Sundays and Kei Rivers near Cape Town. The battles were bloody, and the deaths were many. The second band of European intruders would be more bloodthirsty than the Dutch and would oppress the Africans and the Dutch.

The British also wanted their piece of South Africa, which enraged the Dutch. The Dutch were outmatched in violence and mistreatment by the British. In 1836, tensions between the Voortrekkers (Dutch) and the British resulted in the "Great Trek." Voortrekkers moved northwards in protest against the British policies. The Voortrekkers' "liberation travels" encountered other Indigenous African people, such as the Zulus, which they abused. The Voortrekkers, who purportedly were escaping oppression by the British, oppressed the African populations with which they came in contact. The Voortrekkers eventually pilfered land in the area at or around present-day Pretoria.

During the 19th century, Europeans discovered diamonds near the meeting of the Orange and Vaal rivers. Soon afterwards, gold was found in the Tati area, as alluvial nuggets in the eastern Transvaal and as dust embedded in the rock on the Witswatersrand. These material discoveries caused the Europeans to fight among themselves to tighten their stronghold on South Africa. They would fight and enslave the Africans and one another to build European wealth. Europeans warring among themselves in various wars such as the Anglo-Boer War of 1899–1902 would be bloody and violent. As much as they were aggressive, they became more diabolical to all non-European peoples. They treated the Indigenous Africans horrifically. The demented acts of white supremacy and white terrorism only made the desire for liberation stronger among the oppressed Natives.

In 1912, a group known as the South African Native National Congress (SANNC), later called the African National Congress (ANC), emerged to challenge white supremacist ideology and its outgrowth, the politics of Apartheid. The SANNC chose to utilize its historical origins of Indigenous land inhabitants to organize. They became a group of provincial native congresses and a South African Native Convention whose protest against the decisions of the White National Convention of 1909 had received a modicum of recognition. However, the actions of the ANC and its offshoot groups, such as the Inkatha Freedom Party and the Pan Africanist Congress, spawned many revolts and rebellions by the many Indigenous African and Indian peoples of South Africa.

Of note are how violent actions of the Europeans impacted the entire nation, as evidenced by the Sharpeville Revolt of March 21, 1960, which occurred after the Sharpeville Massacre in the Indigenous African Township of Transvaal. It is reported that the revolt resulted in the police killing 69 Africans and wounding 180 others. The Africans attempted to have a peaceful protest against the white supremacists; however, this was met with brutal violence by the Europeans, which became known as the Sharpeville Massacre. As a result, an armed group of the ANC was formed, which was *uMkonto we Sizwe,* meaning The Spear of the Nation. Nelson Mandela co-founded the group after the ANC was banned following their resistance against the Europeans.

Violent revolts would continue for years. In the 1970s, a revolt by students of the Southwestern Township (SOWETO) over being forced to be taught utilizing a Creole Dutch language of Afrikaans caught the nation's attention and the world's. The Soweto uprising of 1976, which came on the heels of a new Black Consciousness Movement in South Africa, inspired Steven Biko. He ignited flames of revolts and rebellions throughout South Africa. During the Soweto Uprising, more than 20,000 school-aged children protested, and the white-run government killed more than seven hundred.

The actions of the white people of South Africa allowed the world to take notice and take action against Apartheid. As businesses worldwide began to divest their economic interests in South Africa and the people protested

Apartheid, the South African government was forced to rethink many of its racist policies. After many years of bloodshed, the 1990s saw a new democratic system of government emerge. In April 1994, the first democratic elections were held. Nelson Mandela, a formerly imprisoned Indigenous African activist with the ANC, was elected as the President of South Africa from its inception. This led to a Government of National Unity whose responsibility was to draft a new constitution that embraced the cultural and ethnic backgrounds of all the people of South Africa, becoming what is called the Rainbow Nation.

The "Rainbow Nation" of South Africa continues to be deeply engaged in the process of healing from the Apartheid era and before. Centuries of the horrific treatment of the Indigenous Africans by the demented and diabolical Europeans will take years to heal. However, change is a work in progress. There is more acknowledgement of the value of the land's original inhabitants, as seen in the Indigenous concept of Ubuntu (profound humanism) being utilized as the guiding principle post-Apartheid South Africa. Furthermore, it is recognized that South Africa must use South African wisdom (axiology and cosmology) to heal from the evils of the Europeans because the Indigenous populations have a sense of humanity that has not been found to exist among the European tyrants (mention Truth and Reconciliation).

Zulu Cosmology and Axiology

Cosmology alludes to how people organize the universe. This organization consists of family values, beliefs, ethos, and traditions. Axiology refers to the values of a given people. Observing people's values informs one about what is essential to a given people. The true values can be determined by examining the nomenclature, ritual, and traditions of a people. For example, the word Zulu means God's people or people of heaven. Implicit in the name is the true belief of the people; that is, God is central and they (the Zulu) are divine. This alludes to the profound spiritual element that informs the Zulu notion of what has been called the transmission of knowledge and human relations.

Zulu Cosmology

Depending on the context and connotation utilized, God's names are different names among the Zulus. At times God is referred to as *uMvelingqangi* or first Creator; at other times, uNkulunkulu means the Great Grandfather. When *uMvelingqangiis* used, it suggests that all that exists is an extension of one True Source. It implies that *uMvelingqangi* is in everything and is everything. The Zulu concept of *Umoya* (breath) is instrumental within the notation of a god concept. The Zulu suggests that *uMvelingqangi* placed *umoya*—breath, soul, or spirit—in various forms of animals, natural humans, and supernatural beings.

Such a belief would suggest that the Zulus are animistic and advocate polytheism and animism within the Western context. This notion of the breath of the Creator inhabiting all creation is not truly animistic but speaks to that which unifies all people and imbues all people with life. This means that *uMvelingqangi* is being revered as it inhabits that which has been created.

The utilization of *uNkulunkulu* or Great Grandfather speaks to another dimension or manifestation of the God-Force. It implies that God is a nurturer and a provider filled with wisdom, knowledge, and understanding. *uNkulunkulu*, in this regard possesses deep knowledge of all things and the universe. Therefore, like a great grandfather, uNkulunkulu cares for Its family members while providing them with insight, correction, love, and protection. This recognition of the god-force asserts among the Zulus that one must know the Knower and the Provider if one is to know and be provided for. Therefore, one must know *uNkulunkulu*, the unifying force among the Zulu.

It must be noted that there is a quasi-hierarchy within the Zulu cosmological and ontological concept of being with the God-Force occupying the higher position. The ancestors, followed by the elders, are next to *uMvelingqangi*. The ancestors or the ancestral spiritual shades are called *amadlozi or abaphansi*. A literal translation of *abaphansi* is our soil. This suggests that the ancestors are essential to our existence in that they are the foundation upon which we rest, and they provide us with substance. All life grows and is supported by the soil as it interacts with the sun, the rain, and all of the elements of the universe.

The other name for ancestors is *amadlozi*. This word translates into many spirits or many transcendental beings. It suggests that community is essential for physical life. Still, it is so for life beyond what is called physical, meaning that the foundation for a community is filled with mutual aid, respect, and personal accountability. The Zulu suggests that the part of self that is in contact with the physical and spiritual realm during one's physical life is called *ena* (mystic shadow/shade). The *Zulus* believe that each person is simultaneously physically here and beyond the physical realm. The *amadlozi/abaphansi* are very important to the existence of the Zulus. Due to their pivotal role in the community, the *amadlozi/abaphansi* must be appeased. They inform the community when it is time for certain rituals. Rituals are most important within the Zulu cycle.

Rituals *(umisebenzi)* keep people connected to their true Source of life. Through it, one has a set of behaviors to exhibit that will lead to one experiencing an optimal life. When ritual (*umsebenzi*) is not followed correctly, the *amadlozi/abaphansi* are upset and are the ones who can render harm to the community. Conversely, they also allow good to befall the community through the one's execution of *umsebenzi*. The relationship with the ancestors and through the ancestors with God permeates all beings (Holdstock, 1979).

The *amadlozi/abaphansi* offer suggestions when certain actions should take place, when certain conditions are prevalent or threaten to disrupt people's life activities. One is encouraged to live an honorable life because they know that they too will become an ancestor. Therefore, one wants to be pleasing to those who have gone before them, those around them, and those yet to come. The latter two will help one live, at some level, into perpetuity. The goal in life then is not only to please the a*madlozi/abaphansi* but also to live in a manner that one is worthy of becoming an *amadlozi* of repute. To do this, one must please the *amadlozi/abaphansi* and live according to the *uMvelingqangi/uNkulunkulu.*

Reverence for the *amadlozi/abaphansi* is central to experiencing good health and balance within one's life. Balance or *hlelo* (harmony) is a key concept (Ngubane, 1977), and the harmony of the land must be maintained in all things if the community is to remain free from illness. It is evident in the Zulu terms of ukuthula (peace), *ukulinganisa* (balance), *ingqikithi* (essence and context), and *ubunhlobonhlobo* (diversity in all its relatedness). These concepts, as mentioned earlier, being utilized by the Zulus as high ideals, indicate their value to the Zulu.

The cosmos is seen as an undivided universe where plants, animals, humans, ancestors, earth, sky, air, sun, moon, and stars all co-exist in a varying state of balance between order and harmony, disorder and chaos by the Zulus (Ngubane, 1977). Within it is peace, harmony, and balance. All things are a part of the universal whole. The universe is conceptualized as composed of complementary forces that co-exist to inspire growth, development, and movement. The masculine and feminine, male and female, and positive and negative provide dynamism within life. True power is manifested when these forces express themselves correctly and at the proper time.

This concept of balance is evidenced in the relationship between *uNkulunkulu and Nomkhubulwana.*

As mentioned earlier, *uNkulunkulu* is the Great Grandfather, Lord of the sky, responsible for thunder and lightning. *Nomkhubulwana* is his daughter, the virgin princess responsible for the soft, misty spring rain and fertilization of the crops. So here we have harmonizing forces, *Ihlelo* (balance/order), established in the universe.

Even though there is the Great Grandfather who knows and provides, he needs the assistance of the feminine aspect of himself (assuming the child came from him as his seed) to ensure that what he knows is delivered peacefully. The concept of rain and mist can be viewed as soothing, enhancing, and life sustaining, further showing that the idea of balance is supposed to be sacred to the Zulu community.

Umphakathi (community) is most important within Zulu *isintu* (culture). To illustrate the sacredness of *umphakathi*, the Zulu advanced terms such as Ubuntu (humanism), *ubunye* (communalism), and *simunye* (sense of community). Ubuntu will be discussed more fully later in this book. For African life, the community is seen as essential. In addition to the terms mentioned above, the Zulu have to promote strength in the community; they have many proverbs that reiterate this position. One proverb states "*umuntu ngumuntu ngabantu*," or "a person is a person through the other." This means that people must have other people to exist and manifest the essence of personhood.

To express oneself is contingent upon other people's existence to receive and respond to one's expressions of self. Without others, the self-expression would be void of meaning and purpose. The proverb also reminds the Zulus that a person exists because others have existed. If others had not been, then they would not be. It further informs them of indebtedness to those who have gone before them to allow them to be here and to those yet to come who will come to be through them.

Moreover, it suggests that others will continue to exist to the extent that one extends life to those waiting to come into this physical space. We exist as a portal for perpetuity. People are essential to *umphakathi* (community).

Each being is seen as an integral part of the community, with each person possessing some unique personal attributes. Each person has a *khona* (presence) or an uBukhona (universal being) that is imbued with *umphefeumulo* (breath/soul)and *umoya* (breath/spirit).

One's *khona* is revealed in their *ukwenzakomuntu* (human behavior), *unbudlewae* (relationships), *ukuzwa* (experience), and *ulimior isinu* (language or cultural practices). These latter human activities are ways that the *khona* (presence) manifests. One's existence is predicated on one being connected to the community's God-force, ancestors, and persons. Their obligation is to that yet-to-come. One stays connected through conducting rituals, among other things.

On Ubuntu and Life

Ubuntu alludes to something greater than just simply humanism. It suggests that your humanness is intricately tied to my humanness and that we can only be human together. It speaks to honesty, integrity, responsibility, accountability, empathy, caring about others, love, forgiveness, consensus, gratitude, respect for people and property, safety, chastity, valor, humaneness, and communalism.

At the June 1994 graduation of The University of Zululand, King Goodwill Zwelithini stated: "When we describe people as having Ubuntu, we mean that they have a conscience and verve not to disappoint their Creator and those who." The latter left them the heritage of nature, of the beauty of the soil, of the sea and the sky. His statement illustrates the depth of the connection of all things and our responsibility to the Creator (*uMvelingqangi*) and the ancestors *(amadlozi/abaphansi*).

This communal construct allowed King Shaka Zulu to unify the Zulu in 1840 and allowed the Zulu to conceptualize a profound healing system. According to the South African Nobel Laureate Archbishop Desmond Tutu, Ubuntu is described in the following way:

> It is the essence of being human. It speaks that my humanity is caught up and is inextricably bound up in yours. I am human because I belong. It speaks about wholeness; it speaks about compassion. A person with Ubuntu is welcoming, hospitable, warm and, generous, willing to share. Such people are open and

> available to others, willing to be vulnerable, affirm others, and do not feel threatened that others are able and good. They have a proper self-assurance from knowing that they belong in a greater whole. They know that they are diminished when others are humiliated, diminished when others are oppressed, and diminished when others are treated as if they were less than who they are. The quality of Ubuntu gives people resilience, enabling them to survive and emerge still human despite all efforts to dehumanize them.

The concept of Ubuntu is most powerful and must be attended to if one is to have an optimal life. Thus the term sets the standards for human conduct. Unfortunately, within the Western educational system, one will find an absence of this idea of mutual accountability. This story illustrates Ubuntu among children and gives insight into how this concept in education will make a difference in academic performance.

There was an anthropologist who had been studying the habits and culture of a remote African tribe. He had been working in the village for quite some time, and the day before he was to return home, he put together a gift basket filled with delicious fruits from around the region and wrapped it in a ribbon. He placed the basket under a tree, and then he gathered up the children in the village.

The man drew a line in the dirt, looked at the children, and said, "When I tell you to start, run to the tree, and whoever gets there first will win the fruit." They all took their hands and ran together to the tree when he told them to run. Then they sat together around the basket and enjoyed their treat as a group. The anthropologist was shocked. He asked why they would all go together when one of them could have won all the fruits for themselves. A young girl looked at him and said, "How can one of us be happy if all the others are sad?"

References

Holdstock, T. L. (1979). Indigenous healing in South Africa: A neglected potential. *South African Journal of Psychology, 9*(3-4), 118–124. https://doi.org/10.1177/008124637900900308

Ngubane, H. (1977). *Body and mind in Zulu medicine: An ethnography of health and disease in Nyuswa-Zulu thought and practice.* Academic Press.

PART ONE

The Author's Story

"He who does not know can know from learning."
–African Proverb

Researcher's Story

Who Am I?

I WAS BORN ALECIA NICHOLE BLACKWOOD in a small farming district in Jamaica, West Indies. I grew up with solid values, which I learned from my family. My grandparents instilled the values of love, care, respect, integrity, and the importance of getting an education was paramount.

Education was a priority, although my grandparents had basic primary education. They made sure my siblings and I had access to education. At the age of 3, I attended a small prekindergarten school in the town. I distinctly remember my grandad teaching me how to write my name and hold a pencil correctly. My grandparents often shared riddles with us and told us Anansi stories at night. Reading was valued in the house. My granddad would buy the newspaper daily, and we had a small bookshelf with some tattered books that members of our community would borrow from regularly. My grandparents also taught us how to cook, farm, and count money during the summer months. For example, my cousins and I were given a small plot of land to plant vegetables every summer. We learned how to take care of the plants, and when the items were ready, we prepared a meal with vegetables and beans for the family. My grandmother was a highly respected member of the community, and she taught us the importance of working together and helping others. My grandma only had a 3rd-grade formal education. Still, I recalled her teaching elders in the community how to read from a children's book. The only books I saw my grandmother reading were ABC books, children's books, and the Bible. She was known in the community as a loving and caring person. The adults who did not know how to read felt comfortable coming to my grandmother for reading lessons. Furthermore, one day, a native Indian woman (*Taino*) came from a neighboring town to get books from my grandmother to help the people in her village. These are just some examples of sharing and caring I observed growing up.

Primary Education

I spent 6 years in primary school in Jamaica, but 40 years later, I only remember the not-so-good experiences with teachers and students. I am sure I had some fun experiences, but unfortunately, the sad memories outlast the good ones.

I grew up in a rural district and had to walk about 3 miles daily to the town school. I loved learning, but I was a struggling reader! I remember feeling scared of making a mistake in phonics class. For example, one teacher had a big black leather belt with the words "DO THE RIGHT THING" written on it. The teacher used the belt for corporal punishment. I was scared to make a mistake in reading and math class because the teacher would hit us with the belt in the palm of our hands when the answers were incorrect.

Reading was challenging for me. It would take me a long time to finish a book. Honestly, I remember feeling pain in my chest because I could not read some of the words, but I kept it a secret from everyone. It took me a long time to read an entire book, and sometimes, I had to reread it to comprehend the concepts. I also remember how some of us were mistreated by teachers. For example, some children were treated differently by teachers at school based on the town they were from and how they looked and dressed. So, yes, I was paying attention to these things because my uniforms and book bag were not the same quality as the other students.

In grade 2, I had a plan to help all the poor students in the class. My mother at the time was working abroad, and she would send yearly shipments of food, supplies, and other miscellaneous items to my grandmother. When the food, toys, and books shipments arrived, I would be so excited. So, one day, I decided to share the joy with other children I deemed "poor" in my 2nd-grade class. I filled my school bag with many items and gave them away to children I felt did not have much and were poorly treated by the teachers and others. Although I did not get permission to give away the things, I felt deep satisfaction sharing the items with the children at school. Unfortunately, my sense of sharing the joy with the community was short-lived because I was in big trouble when my family found out. Nevertheless, I learned a valuable lesson later that day. Although it was a good thing to share with others, I must first get permission.

When I think about this story and how I shared with my friends in school, it shows that I had a sense of Ubuntu rooted in me from a young age. Ubuntu values are universal and evident across cultures. Although we did not call it Ubuntu in Jamaica, the importance of love, care, and a sense of connectedness to the community was evident in my culture.

My purpose in life is to help and inspire others. So I decided to become a teacher to honor my parents and inspire others, but my dreams were almost shattered when I started teaching in a public school in the United States of America.

I almost quit teaching my first year in public school.

When I started teaching in one of Florida's largest urban school districts, I almost quit because classroom management was challenging. It was challenging for me to ensure that the lessons ran orderly and smoothly. During pre-planning week, I received my class roster with 20 students. On the roster, 12 students had labels next to their names, such as students with learning disabilities (SLD), English for speakers of other languages (ESOL), emotional and behavioral disorders (EBD), 504 plan, gifted, homeless, and attention deficit hyperactivity disorder (ADHD). It was a very culturally and linguistically diverse class of students with a range of behavior issues and exceptionalities.

Many of them were from low socioeconomic backgrounds; their reading was below grade level, while some had emotional and behavioral issues. They were unprepared for school most of the time, and I had little support from their families. As a new teacher, I struggled because I did not feel I had learned the requisite skills in my teacher preparation program to meet the diverse needs of my students. Furthermore, my student teaching experience was in an affluent private Montessori school in New York City. The Montessori school was a homogenous population of students. We had minimal behavior issues, and the parents were incredibly involved. Everything ran smoothly, peacefully, and harmoniously. However, it was highly challenging when I started teaching in one of the largest urban school districts. I needed to learn how to deal with diverse students with a range of behaviors in my class while still instructing them effectively.

During my first semester teaching in the inner-city school, students' behavior worsened and the principal pressured me to rectify the situation. She criticized my lack of management skills, but she did not offer any practical assistance. I was left to figure it out on my own. During a random classroom walkthrough, the principal explicitly told me that I needed to "get my act together" in 2 weeks. Nevertheless, I did not "get my act together," so the principal removed me from the classroom. I was crushed! I felt like my dreams of becoming a good teacher were falling apart. I was demoted to paraprofessional and lost my teaching salary.

After sharing my story with a professor, he recommended that I sign up for a workshop on managing diverse students in urban schools. It was the most practical, hands-on, and transformative seminar that I have ever attended. I learned many strategies on how to build a strong classroom family. Most of all, I realized that I must build relationships with the students. I also learned about what it means to be a culturally responsive teacher. This seminar changed how I viewed my students and helped me be a more caring and reflective teacher. The classroom management workshop enabled me to see beyond the deficit model and build meaningful relationships with the students and their families. That experience summarizes a short narrative of part of the early years of teaching in public education.

My lived experience inspired me to write this book. My first year of teaching in a public school was tumultuous! It took many trials and errors to master the arts and science of education because I did not feel effectively prepared to teach culturally and linguistically diverse students after college. However, as the years went by, I continued to hone my skills by reading, reflecting, and attending professional development training.

I would implement it in my teaching practices throughout the years whenever I learned something new. Also, one day a professor, who researched in South Africa, observed my teaching and said to me, "*you teach in the spirit of Ubuntu*." Unaware of Ubuntu's meaning at that time, I went on a quest to understand Ubuntu's philosophical concept and how it had a positive impact on the classroom environment.

The professor's comment on my teaching sparked my curiosity to reflect on my practice deeply. As a reflective educator, I wanted to understand what pedagogical moves I was making in the class for him to make such a statement. Thus I utilized my knowledge of action research for 2 consecutive school years, and I was intentional about the how, the what, and the why of my teaching practice. I completed a self-study as I worked with the same students for 2 years. I continued to grow as a highly effective teacher during those 2 years. When the students took the state exams, they outperformed their counterparts on the standardized assessment in reading and math, and 100% of my students showed academic and social growth. Reflecting on my journey of teaching students in urban schools, I learned that when we create humane learning spaces for our children, they can rise to and even above the standards and meet their academic goals.

Early Years: Reflection

In the early 2000s, I relocated from New York City to escape the traumatic experiences of 9/11; however, reflecting, I unknowingly brought my traumatic experiences and transferred those experiences into my teaching practices. As a result, my experiences were wrapped up in who I was as an educator. It was not until the following year that my teaching skills improved because I attended a workshop on culturally responsive teaching and became more self-aware. To further understand my journey as an educator, I decided to do a self-study during my seventh year of teaching. The goal of the self-study was to understand better what the observers were witnessing in my teaching practices. For example, some of my colleagues refer to my classroom as the "Zen classroom." In addition, many university professors were impressed with my teaching techniques when they visited my class.

As I mentioned earlier, I conducted a self-study with a focus on how culturally responsive teaching strategies impact students' learning. Gay (2010) defined "culturally responsive teaching as using the cultural knowledge, prior experiences, frames of reference and performance styles of ethnically diverse students to make learning encounters more relevant to and effective for them" (p. 31). Although I intentionally used culturally responsive strategies in my class, the observers saw something unique and different in my actions and students. For example, in conversation with one of the professors, he pointed out that the students in my classroom were respectful, compassionate, and had a keen sense of community. In addition, the students were caring, peaceful, and hospitable to each other. The self-study analysis confirmed that as the facilitator of learning, the shifts happened in my practice when

I became more culturally competent. Cultural competence is "the ability to extend oneself, form authentic relationships and understand, communicate, and effectively interact with diverse others" (Ukpokodu, 2016, p. 43).

As facilitators, we must acknowledge the humanity of the students. We must create a safe environment where students are validated, affirmed, and dignified as human beings. Ukpokodu (2016) posited that when we validate others' humanity, we, in essence, validate our humanity. For instance, I taught the students the importance of not devaluing and dehumanizing each other. They learned about the importance of tolerance and respect in the morning meetings. The morning meeting is a structured part of the day where students learn to build a strong classroom community. In the morning meetings, we talk about the concept of Ubuntu. The students are taught to work together through stories, classroom trust-building activities, and role-plays.

What Is Ubuntu?

In its most straightforward meaning, Ubuntu is an African concept from the Bantu languages in Southern Africa, which loosely means humanness (Samkange & Samkange, 1980).

As I have previously stated, Archbishop Desmond Tutu concisely explained Ubuntu when he posited that a person with Ubuntu feels diminished when others are humiliated, oppressed, and treated as less than their human worth. African theologian scholar John Mbiti posited that "Ubuntu means I am because we are; and since we are, therefore I am." In the Western world, we understand the concept of Ubuntu because we see Ubuntu as an all-inclusive worldview with shared values across cultures that encompass care, compassion, empathy, honesty, hospitality, respect, and tolerance (Biraimah,2016; Letseka,2012; Blackwood,2018). The concept of Ubuntu reminds us that, as humans, we are interconnected and what we do directly impacts others. Through the knowledge of Ubuntu, I had a deeper understanding of self. I created learning spaces in which a "community of truth" is practiced and where both the students and I were able to express what Parker Palmer refers to as the "capacity for the connectedness of the heart" (Palmer, 1998, p. 92). To fully understand the "connectedness of the heart," it is incumbent upon us to first understand ourselves and build authentic relationships with others in the spaces that we share. As educators, this is what we are called upon to do in teaching and learning.

Reflection Questions

Throughout this book, you will need a reflection journal/notebook. In your reflection journal, please answer the following questions.

1. What lessons can you learn from my story?
2. How can you use self-reflection to help you grow?

References

Biraimah, K. L. (2016). Moving beyond a destructive past to a decolonized and inclusive future: The role of African universities in the development of a global curriculum. In N. Wane & A. Todd (Eds.), *Decolonial pedagogy: Examining sites of resistance, resurgence, and renewal* (pp. 25–42). Palgrave Macmillan.

Blackwood, A. (2018). *Transformative learning: Improving teachers' cultural competencies through knowledge and practice of Ubuntu pedagogy* [Doctoral dissertation, College of Education and Human Performance]. http://purl.fcla.edu/fcla/etd/CFE0007157

Gay, G. (2010). *Culturally responsive teaching: Theory, research, and practice* (3rd ed.). Teachers College Press.

Letseka, M. (2012). Educating for Ubuntu/botho: Lessons from Basotho indigenous education. In *Open Journal of Philosophy* (Vol. 3, pp. 337).

Palmer, P. J. (1998). *The courage to teach: Exploring the inner landscape of a teacher's life*. Jossey-Bass.

Samkange, S., & Samkange, T. M. (1980). *Hunhuism/Ubuntuism: A Zimbabwean indigenous political philosophy*. Graham Publishing.

Ukpokodu, O. N. (2016). *You can't teach us if you don't know us and care about us*. Peter Lang Verlag. https://doi.org/10.3726/978-1-4539-1901-9

PART TWO

Teaching in the Spirit of Ubuntu

> *"Ubuntu speaks of the very essence of being human. A person with Ubuntu is open and available to others, affirming of others, does not feel threatened that others are able and good, for he or she has a proper self-assurance that comes from knowing that he or she belongs in a greater whole and is diminished when others are humiliated or diminished when others are tortured or oppressed, or treated as if they were less than who they are."*
>
> –Desmond Tutu

What Is Teaching in the Spirit of Ubuntu?

THE UNDERSTANDING OF TEACHING IN the spirit of Ubuntu came out of deep thought. The concept of deep thought is universal among many Africans and is evident in many African cultures. African deep thought is coded in proverbs, metaphors, and stories. *Seba/SBA* is one way of naming deep thought. The term *Seba* first appeared in the Kemet (ancient Egypt) during the 11th dynasty of the middle kingdom. The Greek term Sophia (wisdom) is derived from the ancient Egyptian *Seba*. The term *Seba*, like most *Kemetic* words, is *polysémie*, meaning that it carries other meanings and associations. *Seba* is both a verb and a noun; it is deep thought and deep thinking. *Seba* means teaching, learning, wisdom, and studying; collectively, deep thought. *Seba* can also describe a moral teacher who contemplates morality and the profound meaning of things and teaches through instruction and exemplary practice (Hilliard, 1998).

Teaching in the spirit of Ubuntu has to do with how the teacher connects with the learner to deeply engage them in the learning process. Dr. Wade Nobles refers to this connection as a "spiritual dance"; true education happens when the educator has a deep connection with the learners. When students feel a connection, it ignites their passion for knowledge, motivates them, and inspires a love for learning. Children know when one genuinely cares about them; once they feel authentic love and compassion, they become more motivated to learn. Touching the spirit of the learner requires deep knowledge of self and our place in this world. Knowledge of the Ubuntu pedagogy gives one the techniques to master the humanistic arts and science of teaching while building authentic relationships. Ukpokodu (2016) points out that Ubuntu pedagogy is grounded in the idea that all students are humans, and they can excel if their humanity is placed front and center of their learning. Once the students are at the focal point of our instructions, we then decide on how we are going to use their learning context, learning styles, and instructional strategies to meet their diverse needs. When we acknowledge students' humanity, it opens the door to trust or touching their spirit. Touching the spirit of students can be done whether they are in face-to-face or virtual learning spaces. To touch the students' spirit, we must intentionally validate the learners by building authentic relationships and genuinely showing that we care about the learner.

Ubuntu Pedagogy Versus Traditional Pedagogy

Ubuntu pedagogy offers a different approach than traditional pedagogy. Ubuntu pedagogy focuses on humanizing learning spaces by fostering a partnership between teachers and students as co-creators of knowledge. It promotes mutual respect, care, and affirmation of our shared humanity, emphasizing interconnectedness and collective well-being. This approach values diverse perspectives and experiences, encouraging collaboration and inclusivity. By prioritizing community and relationships, Ubuntu pedagogy seeks to create an environment where every participant feels valued and respected, leading to a deeper engagement and a more meaningful learning experience. The pedagogy incorporates indigenous knowledge systems and cultural practices, which contribute to the learner's holistic development, recognizing the importance of emotional, social, and spiritual growth alongside academic achievement (Letseka, 2012; Ukpokodu, 2016; Blackwood, 2018; Venter, 2004).

In contrast, traditional pedagogy often operates within a hierarchical framework where the teacher is the primary authority and students are passive recipients of knowledge. It tends to be more individualistic and competitive, prioritizing personal achievement over collective success. Traditional methods are typically teacher centered and standardized, offering limited opportunities for authentic collaborative learning (Ukpokodu, 2016). This model of teaching emphasizes rote memorization and standardized testing, often overlooking students' diverse needs and backgrounds (Gay, 2010). It focuses on transmitting a fixed body of knowledge with less emphasis on critical thinking, creativity, and problem-solving skills (Apple, 2004). Traditional pedagogy can sometimes marginalize students who do not fit the conventional mold, failing to acknowledge and leverage their unique strengths and perspectives (Ngubane & Makua, 2022; Dei, 1996). See the comparative chart outlining the key differences between Ubuntu pedagogy and traditional pedagogy from various researchers. This chart includes insights from educational theorists and practitioners who have studied the impacts of both pedagogical approaches on student outcomes, engagement, and overall well-being (see Appendix D).

Conceptual Framework of Ubuntu Pedagogy

Figure 2.1 Conceptual Framework

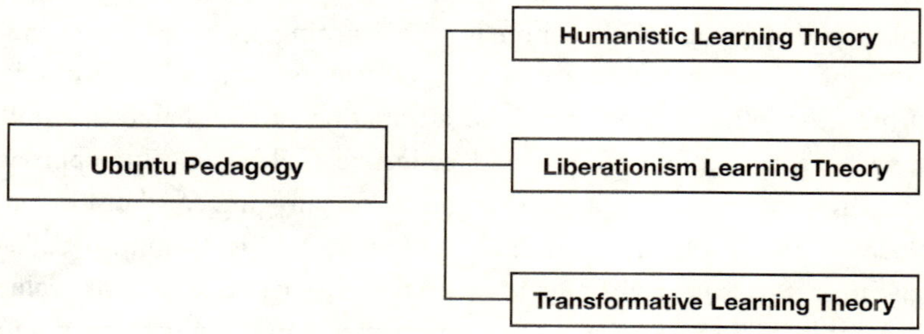

The conceptual framework of Ubuntu pedagogy is supported by humanism learning theories such as liberationism and transformative learning theory. Humanistic learning theory consists of four main areas: human capabilities, creativity, personal growth, and choice.

In humanistic learning theory, Maslow and other humanists support the idea that children are inherently good, and when their needs are met, they are more likely to focus on learning (Bates, 2019). The underpinning of Ubuntu pedagogy is a student-centered approach. It is grounded in the idea that all students can excel if their humanity is placed front and center of the learning. The goal is to help students develop agency. When students build agency, it gives them a voice and an awareness of their education. Student agency is crucial because it fosters self-motivation and builds autonomous learners. It is about empowering students to be self-directed learners who take responsibility for their learning and respect themselves and others (hooks, 2003).

According to Paulo Freire, a Brazilian teacher and education theorist, liberationism learning theory aims to liberate human beings, enabling us to help build a world in which it is easier to see the humanity of each other and work together and care for one another. He believed that students should engage in learning that gives them access to information that will allow them to think critically and free themselves of the system created by the oppressors. Liberatory education is a transformative problem-posing method in which teachers and students are critical co-investigators in the learning process "liberatory pedagogy" (Freire, 1978). The teacher and students are co-investigators because the teacher serves as the facilitator of learning that supports and helps the students to see how the learning connects to their world (Ukpokodu, 2007).

Both the teacher and student have specific roles but work together to create a successful learning journey. One of the primary goals of the socializing process is to help the student be a self-directed learner. The role of the teacher is to be a facilitator of learning that sparks the students' curiosity, builds confidence, motivates the students, and sets clear goals for the students so that they can become autonomous learners.

Students can develop autonomy from an early age when their learning process aligns with goals and plans. The role of a teacher then is that of a guide who monitors, provides effective feedback, and evaluates the learning outcomes. For example, the teacher can monitor the students at an early age by helping to make goals that can range from daily activities to future plans. The teacher should also ask the children questions to evaluate their thinking. One way you can have students assess their thinking is using the prompt "I used to think, but now I know." When students are taught how to evaluate their thinking after a while, it becomes a natural process for them, strengthening their critical thinking skills.

Characteristics of a Self-Directed Learner

Self-directed learners value learning, take the initiative, have self-control, and demonstrate responsibility for learning. They often take control of their education by seeking information beyond what is exposed to them by the teacher. Ultimately, that is where we want all learners to be, actively making choices and decisions about what they are learning and setting clear goals for themselves. These characteristics can be developed if students are in a learning environment where they feel safe and secure.

The teacher plays a critical role in fostering self-directed learning. Therefore, the teachers have to promote engagement to inspire students to become self-motivated and self-directed learners. The teachers must be intentional about the learning goals, and the students are the core of all decisions made in the plan of a lesson. Each lesson should incorporate elements of social-emotional learning strategies. Social-emotional learning (SEL) is a process for learning life skills, including dealing with oneself, others, and relationships and how to work effectively.

A safe learning environment is also meaningful because when students feel safe physically, mentally, and emotionally, they can focus on learning.

Letseka (2000) pointed out that a person with Ubuntu characteristics is kind, compassionate, humble, and virtuous and strives to promote peace and harmony. Ubuntu pedagogy promotes a humanizing classroom environment where every child can learn to their maximum potential. Ubuntu pedagogy is anchored by six key components that humanize the teaching and learning process. The six pedagogical strategies of Ubuntu pedagogy are:

- Understanding of self
- Building relationships and setting boundaries
- Unifying the class to work together
- Nurturing the minds of the children
- Teaching from a position of love and care, and
- Utilizing evidence-based practices to meet the diverse needs of all students

Understand Self!

To teach, we must know ourselves. Teaching is a sacred profession with much responsibility and duty towards students. Teachers play an essential role in inspiring students, building students' confidence, and directing them in the right direction. In addition, a teacher plays a significant role in education, helping to cultivate each generation to positively reproduce and refine the best of themselves, passing on the accumulated wisdom, knowledge, and skills to the next generation to build a robust and prosperous future. Therefore, teachers must take time to know themselves. Thus, the first requirement to be a master teacher is to know one's strengths and weaknesses. When we know our strengths and weaknesses, it serves as an asset. It is an asset because it helps us critically reflect, explore our shortcomings, and learn what areas we need to improve.

One can explore oneself by asking questions such as:

- Who is the person at the center of your teaching self?
- Do you bring your true, authentic self into the room?
- Do you have a separate teaching persona?
- Do you strive to make personal connections with your students?
- What are your values?

Make a list of the things you don't know by questioning yourself in your reflection journal. For example:

- I don't know how to have a difficult conversation.
- I want to develop skills in teaching advanced math.
- I don't know how to teach writing to young children.
- Take a moment and explore yourself. What are some of your weaknesses?
- Before you continue reading the chapter, make a list of your weaknesses.
- After you make a list of your weaknesses:
- Read them out loud to yourself.
- Think about which of them you must work on first and then prioritize the list.

Please put them in order of how you plan to work on them; once you identify the most needed areas in your self-development, set goals on how you will work on them. Stepping into your next masterpiece requires selecting practical plans and intentionally working on them. Make a conscious effort to grow by actively working on your goals. As you visualize your aspirations, remember that support can come in unexpected forms—a book you read or wise advice from someone who offers the guidance you need. Keep addressing your weaknesses; growth is not an overnight process. Recognizing these areas will help you navigate challenges when your weaknesses become obstacles to progress.

Identify Your Strengths

If you want to know yourself, it is important to identify your strengths. Your strengths are traits that you are naturally good at doing. Make a list of the things that you do well. What are the things that you can do well? What are the things people applaud you for and encourage you to do?

Another way to explore your strengths is to use social science–researched strength-based tests. Strengths-based tests are online assessments that measure your innate abilities based on how you think, behave, and feel. All strengths-based assessments have a list of strengths that are grouped into categories. Some of the top strength tests are the Teaching Strengths Quiz, Strength Profile, Top 5 Clifton Strengths, High5 Test, VIA, and Character Strengths Survey. Strengths-based tests are other ways of learning about your unique personality. These scientific tests are tools to support your observation of self.

Professor Bayyinah Bello, a Vodouvi Historian, Afro-descendant educator, writer, and humanitarian, uses a holistic approach to help us become more self-aware. She emphasizes a natural method for developing self-knowledge, teaching us to explore the African aphorism "Know thyself." Professor Bayyinah Bello encourages continuous self-reflection through this aphorism. As outlined by her, the seven steps to knowing oneself are understanding Courage, Speaking, Observation, Meditation, Action, Creation, and Being Oneself. These steps encourage individuals to reflect and grow continuously (Bello,2021).

Table 2.1 Know Thyself

Component	Description
1. Courage	Efficient management of our fears
2. Speaking	Using words according to one's own convictions
3. Observation	Accessing specifics of the external world to learn from it
4. Meditation	Focusing on inner observation and debate

5. Action	Acting in harmony with our words and thoughts
6. Creation	Providing tools, realizations, or circumstances that are vital for the community
7. Being Oneself	Establishing greater and greater harmony between one's thoughts, words, and actions

Source: The natural approach of facilitating knowledge of the self by Professor Bayyinah Bello https://bayyinahbello.com/

Utilizing the seven natural approaches for facilitating knowledge of self will help educators discover that divine power within and help the learners understand themselves. Knowledge of self should be cultivated from a young age. Therefore, master teachers must also use opportunities to help their students understand themselves. Knowledge of self is essential in education for both the teacher and the learner. When the learner has self-awareness, it builds their confidence and they can better connect with the subject matter being taught in the lesson. I believe knowledge of self should be integrated into the curriculum used to teach our students.

Furthermore, I have found that having a deeper self-awareness helps promote a more positive attitude when things get challenging as a teacher. For example, we might encounter a problematic child, parent, or colleague, and we have high self-awareness; in these situations, we are more likely to reflect on the problem instead of reacting. We can reflect on the situation by asking ourselves "I wonder what brought this child or person to this place of negativity?" "I wonder how they are feeling at this moment." Pausing to reflect instead of reacting will allow one to address the situation from a calm place rather than committing violence to oneself. When we react without thinking, we create violence first onto ourselves. Reflection also helps to find more restorative solutions.

Cultural Identity

Having a strong cultural identity is an essential part of knowing oneself. It gives us a sense of belonging and connects us to others. Our culture informs our values and interests, which helps to ground our understanding of self, life, and worldview. Cultural identity is a deep understanding of how our values, customs, and traditions shape who we are. A strong sense of our own culture helps to build our cultural competence. Cultural competence is the ability to understand one's own culture and show empathy to others. When we are culturally competent, we understand the uniqueness of other people's cultures and show them respect without judgment. Cultivating our cultural competence allows us to extend ourselves authentically and not feel threatened by others. The goal is to reach a level of Ubuntu competence.

Ubuntu competence is the understanding that our humanity is interconnected with others. In Nguni tradition, Ubuntu is best described in the saying "*umuntu ngumuntu ngabantu,*" meaning a person is a person through others or "I am because we are" (Mbigi, 1997). This African worldview reminds us that we do not exist by ourselves in this world. Our actions and behaviors have a direct impact on others. Therefore, we must be mindful of how we show up in learning spaces. Are our actions and behaviors promoting positivity or negativity? Having Ubuntu competence allows us to operate from a humane place—seeing the humanity in others so that we can fully express compassion, kindness, love, and dignity for other human beings.

One way to explore ourselves is by unpacking our unique social and cultural identities. We can explore our cultural identity by asking, "Who am I?" Before developing cultural knowledge and awareness about others, we must first uncover and examine our personal, social, and cultural identities. Stop and complete the cultural identity activity in Appendix B. Guided self-reflection helps us better understand how culture, traditions, and social context impact who we are. This exercise is an essential vehicle for developing a sense of who we are.

Additionally, knowledge of our strengths, weaknesses, and cultural/worldviews will help us see the humanity in others and connect us to the community of truth, justice, harmony, balance, and reciprocity. Make a list of those things. Stop, breathe deeply, and then write the things down. Do not go to the next page until you write the list. After you make your list, read them aloud. This is an opportunity for you to affirm yourself and validate yourself. Knowing your strengths will help you cultivate the things that come naturally to you. Once you know your strengths, it will help you feel more confident in your abilities.

Building Positive Relationships With Others

The second component of Ubuntu pedagogy is building positive relationships. Positive relationships matter and it is the glue that connects us to the human family. It is responsible for safe and harmonious learning environments where students and teachers respect each other. Developing authentic relationships with others opens the door for learning to take place. Quality learning cannot occur if we do not cultivate genuine relationships with the learner. It is crucial to connect to the spirit of the learner. When learners feel connected, they are more likely to respond to the instruction better. They respectfully show up in the learning spaces, ready to learn.

Image 2.1 Elementary community-building activity called A Spider Web.

Getting to Know Your Students: Elementary community-building activity called A Spider Web.

Community-building activities foster a sense of belonging and nurture a feeling of ownership and accountability in the classroom. With a strong classroom community, the teacher does not have to micromanage the students because they hold each other accountable for their actions.

In addition, the experience of working together to solve problems in play and projects creates an opportunity for children to learn important cooperation skills. It also helps the students build trust among themselves. Community-building activities provide unique opportunities for children to build positive relationships with their peers and create a harmonious environment where they can thrive socially and academically. For example, I shared my story early in the book about why I almost quit teaching. However, I did not share that I was reinstated in the class six weeks later after much growth and development in showing up for myself and the students.

Within three months of being reinstated in the class, I was able to change how I delivered instructions by redesigning the classroom structure and setting clear procedures for the students and myself. Thus, I had a successful school year for the rest of the time. I learned from that situation that building authentic relationships with the students is crucial.

Furthermore, I learned that I must "see my students for learning to take place." Yes, seeing the students means that the educator must be aware of the student. Acknowledging students by name and greeting them before they enter the class is a simple way to show that you respect and dignify them as human beings. A teacher must also get to know each one of the students on a personal level. It is crucial to get to know all the students, whether teaching in person or virtual. Getting to know the students requires that we are intentional with our actions and invest the time in getting to know them on a deeper level. Asking open and honest questions is one way to get to know students deeply and build a strong classroom community. To get to know the students on a deeper level ask them questions such as:

- What do you like?
- What brings you joy?
- What are your favorite foods?
- What is your favorite TV show?
- How are you feeling?
- How was your weekend?

Tell me about the funniest video you saw on social media, or name a song or lyrics that describe how you feel. Teachers can actively engage the students by asking questions before starting a lesson. For example, teachers can incorporate the question at the elementary level during their morning meetings. Teachers can also get to know the students by playing educational games; bringing real-world experience changes how the students respond to learning.

At the secondary and university level, an educator can get to know the students by creating a video to welcome the students to the class and sending welcoming emails, addressing students by their names, providing detailed feedback to each individual, and learning the names of all the students. These are examples of what teachers can ask students to get to know them and build a strong classroom community. All teachers from elementary to higher education levels are encouraged to know the students. Asking questions, playing trust games, and allowing students to share about themselves are all opportunities to get to know them deeply. It strengthens the relationships among the students. Building rapport with students helps them be more invested and connected to the learning process.

Building relationships gives a sense of belonging and connectedness. Researchers show that no significant learning occurs with students without effective relations. Students learn best when they have a sense of personal connection and feel the instructor cares about them. It sends a powerful message to the children that they matter. It does not matter their color or creed; when we take the time to affirm, validate, and dignify them, it shows them how to love and care for each other. It empowers the children to develop positive self-esteem, confidence, respect, and positive relationships with others. In essence, we teach them the power of love.

Unifying Students to Work Together

Teaching students to love and care for each other is another powerful way to build a strong classroom community. Teachers can demonstrate love through actions, telling stories with morals, and being consistent and fair with expectations for all students.

Building a solid classroom community requires educators to be mindful of behaviors in and out of the classroom. Students pay close attention to the behavior and mannerisms of their teachers. They will emulate the conduct, whether it is good or bad. For example, if a teacher is sarcastic, many of the students will also demonstrate sarcastic behaviors. Similarly, if a teacher has a kind and warm demeanor, the students will also demonstrate that warmer demeanor vibe among themselves and others.

Students get their cues of social behavior from their teachers. They learn about good or bad behavior from their teacher's actions and words. Students pay close attention, listen deeply to our words, and watch our behavior to see if they match ours. So, if we err, we must humble ourselves and use it as an opportunity to teach. When we are wrong, we must humble ourselves and apologize; it shows that we too are imperfect and can learn from our mistakes.

Taking the time to self-reflect and having honest conversations with children about their feelings teaches them empathy. Empathy leads them to see and feel for others. Promoting collective empathy and compassion strengthens the classroom relationship with others and encourages respect.

Stories and biographies with messages of perseverance, endurance, love, and trust are ways to strengthen the relationships among the students. Folktales are another wonderful way to build their confidence and show them empathy for others around them. When students are confident in their abilities, it builds up their resilience, and they are more likely to persevere through challenges.

Our students come to us from different walks of life with sometimes different experiences, hidden biases, and prejudices; therefore, we must intentionally teach them to unpack their feelings toward others. But remember, we first have to explain it to ourselves so that when we teach them to be hospitable, compassionate, and empathetic, we are transparent in our mindset.

Nurture the minds of the students.

When we nurture children's minds, we show them that we deeply care and that caring action empowers them and contributes to their development. Working with children requires putting them at the center of the decision making. Furthermore, the design and delivery of instruction should consider the students' social-emotional needs. The teacher's responsibility is to be very aware and connect with each learner's intellect, humanity, and spirit. Caring teachers genuinely look out for their students' best interests and set high expectations for each student. Caring teachers also create safe learning spaces in which learners can build their confidence and work to their maximum potential.

Care is an action word; therefore, it is not about what we say; it must be followed up by doing something. So, for example, if we tell students that we care about their academic success, an actionable thing would be to provide support to them when they begin to struggle. That support can be taking time to help the students or referring them to others who can help.

Teach from a position of love and care.

I have learned in my years of teaching that caring has to be genuine. Care cannot be fake! Teachers must care genuinely for students and show them love! Teachers cannot fake being compassionate! Young learners are apt to identify fakeness once they interact with that teacher. Some learners appear to have a radar to detect fakeness. The students always have a way to spot a fake teacher and thus challenge their authority. Therefore, I encourage all teachers to examine themselves before working with students. To nurture students' minds, I encourage all teachers to bring their caring selves to the learning spaces.

We must have good heart habits. Heart habits are dispositions intended to help people develop their social-emotional intelligence. They are emotional dispositions that help people care for each other, honor others, and respect the emotions and rights of others and how they see the world.

Habits of mind and heart can help shift people's mindsets in a school. Habits of mind and heart are mental habits students can cultivate and develop to render their thinking to help self-regulate their emotions. Students who can control their thoughts and manage their feelings are more receptive to learning. Therefore, students must be taught how to control their feelings early. In addition, teachers must teach students problem-solving and life-related skills necessary to help them operate effectively in society. For example, we must ensure the stories we share with the students are relatable and relevant to their world. As a result, we have shifted our mindset and made meaningful connections with our students.

Furthermore, to ensure that students stay actively engaged and focused on learning, teachers must skillfully use strategies that will challenge the students to think and communicate with clarity and precision. When we challenge students to think about their thinking (metacognition), it sometimes leads to frustration. However, a master teacher must also help students manage their frustration emotions by skillfully observing, listening, and understanding empathy and scaffolding the instructions to support the learner. I refer to this as "the spirit dance" in teaching. Actively observing, deeply listening, and checking for understanding with empathy are techniques teachers can use to make instructional adjustments in a lesson to support the learner.

Teachers need to learn more about the students' cultural context and use that information to help them see themselves in the curriculum. When students share their cultural norms with us, it's our duty as teachers to facilitate a safe learning environment where the students feel confident showing up being their authentic selves. Creating a safe learning space is paramount to learning. Students who don't feel valued and respected are less likely to learn.

As educators, we must be intentional about humanizing the curriculum. We must approach teaching and learning from a humanistic standpoint because the curriculum is used to help socialize students. Validating and respecting students is the first step in humanizing the learning environment. A humane classroom is a place where students feel warmly seen and safe. Letting the students know you see them and they are not invisible is crucial for teaching face to face or online. In such an environment, our students are far more likely to be eager to learn and to persist in learning. Another way to humanize the classroom is to explicitly teach and model what respect sounds like and looks like in practice. For instance, the teacher can share stories, songs, and dialogues centered around respect to cultivate a culture of respect in the class. Examples can be based on something that happened at school or relevant to the student's social context.

At the elementary level, the teachers can discuss respect and create posters of what was discussed in the class. Here is an example of a poster about respect:

Figure 2.2 Anchor Chart about Respect.

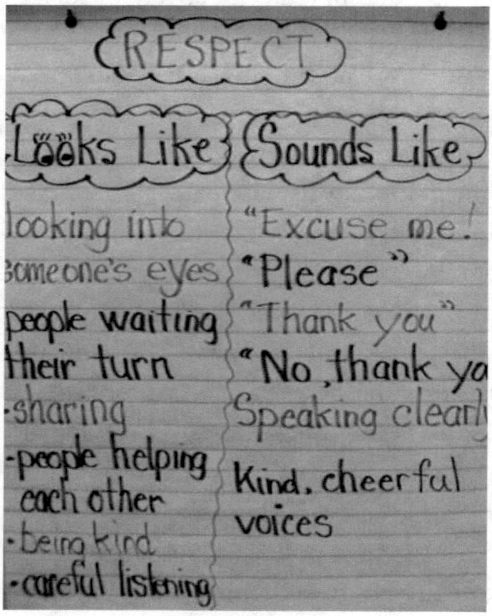

Source: Anchor Chart about Respect. (n.d.). *Classroom Collective.* https://classroomcollective.tumblr.com/

Utilizing evidence to evaluate the growth and development of all learners.

It is important to create a learning space that fosters and promotes mutual respect amongst the students, whether in person or virtual. Furthermore, teachers should also:

- Have high regard for the students
- Be a model of what respect looks like and sounds like
- Show students that they are in control of their thoughts and actions

Therefore, teachers must set clear expectations and boundaries in the classrooms. They must be patient in explaining, modeling, and reteaching students how to conduct themselves. Teachers must practice self-control and let students feel empowered in the classroom. A teacher must never try to overpower students by using fear and punishment to get them to do a task. Students must understand from an early age that they must have self-control. Teach them how their good or bad choices affect them and others around them. For example, let them know that we are all teachers in a learning space. Therefore, when the teacher is speaking, everyone must listen. Likewise, when their classmates are speaking, it is essential to show respect and listen deeply because, at that moment, they are the teacher. The goal is to show the students that in our learning environment, power is shared. This concept promotes mutual respect in a classroom.

Another way to humanize the curriculum is to validate all students' cultural and linguistic diversity in the class. Diversity is the ability to recognize and respect people's differences. Our students' social identities, personalities, cognitive skills, athletic abilities, socio-emotional well-being, home environments, and the like will influence how they bring themselves to the classroom context. If viewed positively, the challenges associated with student diversity can lead to a more supportive and motivating classroom experience.

As teachers, we must acknowledge cultural diversity and make sure the students' culture is incorporated in all curriculum areas, including language arts, mathematics and science, and history. When students' cultures are included, it creates an inclusive and equitable learning environment. Inclusivity involves understanding and utilizing our knowledge of students' lived experiences and the communities they belong to in order to connect with them and develop curricular activities that speak to their unique experiences. When students feel seen and heard and are given agency in their learning, they are more likely to succeed in your classroom. In addition, equitable learning environments feel fair to students, where no matter what is occurring in their lives, they can expect to receive the assistance they need to succeed academically.

Humanizing the curriculum means being intentional about our teaching practices so that students feel seen, safe, and respected. If we are to develop children with solid self-efficacy and morals, we have to be deliberative about the social and cultural context to which we expose them. Additionally, we must embrace a learning environment that embraces diversity and is highly thoughtful about humanizing the classroom experience for themselves and their students.

A humanized classroom environment is one where students feel free to be authentic and show vulnerability. To achieve this goal, we must respect each other and continue incorporating students' lived experiences and cultures into the learning environment. Teach from a position of love and care. Love and care are prerequisites for teaching, which is held in high regard in traditional African culture. A teacher must also understand how to connect with the learner's spirit.

Teaching is a spiritual dance that touches the essence of the being. When students feel the love and respect from the teacher, they reciprocate that love and spread it amongst each other. Love is a trauma-informed strategy that calms the brain. Neuroscientist Ken Ginsburg explained that when young people have been exposed to adverse childhood experiences, they are often in a "fight or flight" mode, but constantly being exposed to love and a caring environment confuses the amygdala. Even brain science confirms what I have known to be true, working with marginalized and disenfranchised communities for many years. I have seen how teaching love and exposing children to authentic love and care has helped change their mindset and help them build resilience. Resilience is the inner strength that helps one overcome challenges despite past and current challenges in life. When students are exposed to a loving and caring teacher, it positively affects their lives. A caring teacher can make a difference in the lives of students. Caring teachers go above and beyond what is required of them to ensure their students are confident socially and academically. Teaching from a position of care requires that the teacher knows the cultural context and uses that information as an asset in building a positive learning environment. For example, if a teacher does not live in the community they teach, they must get a community tour to learn more about the land and people. The tour can be virtual or in person. The community tour aims to help the teacher connect with the community's human aspect and adopt a strength-based teaching approach. The teacher can then use the information to connect them with the learners. When students see themselves in the curriculum, they are more connected to the teaching and learning process. Creating hospitable learning spaces where students feel safe and ready to learn is the ultimate goal of touching the whole child.

Teaching is an active process. To ensure that the learners master the information presented, the teachers must continue learning about each student and use evidence-based practices to evaluate the teaching and learning process. Getting to know your students on all levels, academically and socially, helps improve achievement. Teachers must study their students by using evidence from the teaching and learning to ensure that they are meeting the diverse needs of the students. For example, the teacher can monitor the students' progress, collect data, and use the information to inform the lesson. Teachers must collect data on the students daily. The data collection does not have to be a formal process such as a diagnostic or summative assessment but rather an observation and checking for understanding. The data collection should be an ongoing process that helps teachers make conscientious decisions before, during, and after teaching. The multiple data sources will help the teacher provide the students with the most relevant instructions. For example, educators must be intentional about getting to know their students on a social and academic level, whether they have 5 or 50 students. How do I get to know my students? When I receive the roster of new students, I examine their school records to get background information about each student. The structure of the classroom is designed with the students in mind. Once I meet the students, I ask them personal questions, and I use that information to inform my instruction and further build relationships with them. Furthermore, I closely monitor my students' data and create an academic prescription card for every child. An *academic prescription card* is a written document that provides an in-depth narrative of the strengths and weaknesses of each student. The prescription card is an interactive, ongoing progress monitoring tool that shows students' academic and social progress. I use the cards to facilitate discussions with the students and their families. We discussed the students' successes and what they would like to improve regarding their performance during the student-led conference.

Observational data is another way to learn about students. The teaching and learning process is not linear; it is cyclical. The facilitator of learning must constantly reflect on the plan and make the necessary adjustments to the context they are teaching. It is essential to adjust instructional strategies based on culture, context, and the student's learning styles. Studying children that we work with is very important. If we work with them in person or a virtual environment, we must work hard to get to know the learners on all levels so that we can meet their diverse needs.

Furthermore, all teachers must understand how learning works and how knowledge is transferred. Research shows that information must be transferred from short-term to long-term memory for learning to occur. If learners have more than seven pieces of information in their short-term memory at one time, they get an overload. To prevent cognitive overload, educators must prioritize the information they give students. The information must be broken into chunks with clear learning goals. This type of instructional strategy can be done with kindergarten to college students. Once the teacher presents a clear learning goal, they must get the student's attention and help them connect with new material and what they already know.

One strategy to help students process what they learn is to present the information and give them opportunities to discuss what they know with their peers. When students actively engage in dialogue about the information, it allows them to move the information from their short-term memory into their long-term memory. In addition, when students work in groups to talk about the information, it allows them to take more responsibility for their learning and deepen their understanding.

Giving students assessments is another way to evaluate the learning process and determine whether the students demonstrate mastery and are ready for the next level of instruction. The purpose of the assessment is to allow students to show what they learn about the content in class. It is an effective technique for evaluating a student's knowledge regarding a subject matter.
After each assessment, students are given feedback. The immediate feedback provides the students with an accurate understanding of academic level, strengths, and areas for improvement. Furthermore, the students are afforded

opportunities to represent and demonstrate their knowledge of the content in multiple ways, including multimedia, videos, and various technologies to help engage students in the learning process. When a student is assigned a task, it is important to explicitly model the expectation and provide clear instructions regarding the most effective way to complete the task.

Why Is Ubuntu Pedagogy Necessary for the 21st Century and Beyond?

The education of our children is paramount in developing and establishing a secure future. The Ubuntu Pedagogy framework is a perfect antidote to revolutionizing how we educate children. Asante (2017) reminds us in the book *Revolutionary Pedagogy* that we must seek to overturn ordinary thinking, methods, and practices of creating and delivering knowledge to children. We must explore different teaching and thinking methods so that all learners understand their role in this world.

The current public education system in America is not set up for Black and minority children to succeed. Black and minority children are at the bottom of the Nation's Report Card on academic achievement. Our Black and Brown children perform significantly below average based on their standardized measures. We understand this is a complex problem with many contributing factors, but humanism in the curriculum must be explored. Is the curriculum humanizing? Is it culturally relevant? Are the educators teaching from a position of love and care? Are the learning environments safe and affirming? Education is designed to socialize our children. Therefore, it must prepare all learners to have a strong cultural identity and help them to understand who they are and their purpose in this world.

The collective traumas that our children have experienced for generations must be counteracted with a pedagogy that puts their humanity first. Ubuntu-oriented teaching style calls for us to affirm, dignify, and validate every child that comes into our learning space. We must teach the mind, body, and spirit of the child. Therefore, it requires that we, the educators, the facilitators of learning, know ourselves and build authentic relationships with the children to help nurture their minds.

True education is about touching the spirit of the child. It is a spiritual dance between the learner and the teacher. The teacher is the facilitator to help the learner activate what is within. Teaching is both a science and an art, and it requires educators to be aware of themselves and the best instructional practices to meet the diverse needs of all learners.

Teachers must constantly upgrade their skills to ensure that learners are prepared with the skill sets to help them navigate the 21st century and beyond. One writer refers to skills students would need to navigate successfully life in the 21st century as the 4 C's-:

1. Collaboration
2. Communication
3. Creativity, and
4. Critical thinking skills

The writer pointed out that broad skills are the primary tools to help our children succeed in the 21st century and beyond. With our growing and ever-changing world, we do not just rely on basic limited skill sets; we must teach broad skill sets to prepare students to be deep, innovative thinkers to solve tomorrow's problems. The educator has to facilitate and create opportunities for deeper learning to prepare children for the future. I refer to these educators as Ubuntu-responsive educators. An Ubuntu-responsive educator (URE) understands self, affirms, dignifies, and validates others by first acknowledging the humanity of the learner before teaching the content. An Ubuntu-responsive educator extends help to students beyond the call of duty. They care deeply about the success of the students. They create learning spaces that are welcoming and inclusive of the students' culture and social context; they also provide books and artifacts to which the students can relate and support the students based on their individual needs.

Furthermore, Ubuntu-responsive educators set high expectations for all students by scaffolding the instructions so that the students can reach their goals. They also help students set goals and encourage them to work towards them. Finally, UREs value how much students learn and grow, so they go above and beyond to find resources to support their students.

Ubuntu-responsive educators understand how to create classroom communities where the students feel affirmed and validated. An Ubuntu-responsive educator understands how to design learning spaces where the students work together like a family unit and strong partnerships are developed with the parents or guardians of the children. They build trusted relationships with the families and work together for the child's success. For example, UREs care deeply about their students and ensure that students' social-emotional needs are met. For instance, if students need personal hygiene items, they provide them. Sometimes these teachers also show interest in the students outside of the school.

For example, they often attend a student's game, birthday party, recital, or other significant events in the child's life. When teachers extend themselves, it shows that they deeply care about their students. This act of kindness builds lasting relationships for life with the learners.

An Ubuntu-responsive educator can be a parent; remember, the parents are the first teachers. For instance, a parent with a written plan and a clear mission and vision statement for their child/ren is considered an Ubuntu-responsive educator. The parent educator knows their child or children and has a clear plan for the children's success.

A parent who teaches their children morals, the value of culture and community, and how to love and care for each other is considered an Ubuntu-responsive educator. Ubuntu-responsive educators do not spoil their children. When the children err, they discipline them with love and care and use the misbehavior as an opportunity to teach. Ubuntu-responsive parent educators teach children to respect life and the importance of taking care of the environment in which they live. The children also learn to show respect to those who came before them, their elders, parents, brothers and sisters, and themselves. They also learn about the importance of having good character.

Reflection Questions

1. In what ways do you help students?
2. Are you an Ubuntu-responsive educator?
3. Can you explain how you incorporate Ubuntu principles in your teaching?

References

Apple, M. W. (2004). *Ideology and curriculum* (3rd ed.). Routledge.

Asante, M. K. (2017). *Revolutionary pedagogy: Primer for teachers of Black children*. Africa World Press.

Bates, B. (2019). *Learning theories simplified: ... and how to apply them to teaching* (2nd ed.). Sage Publications.

Bello, B. (2021). *Know yourself course*. Bayyinah Bello. Retrieved July 1, 2024, from https://bayyinahbello.com/

Blackwood, A. (2018). *Transformative learning: Improving teachers' cultural competencies through knowledge and practice of Ubuntu pedagogy* [Doctoral dissertation, College of Education and Human Performance]. http://purl.fcla.edu/fcla/etd/CFE0007157

Dei, G. J. S. (1996). *Anti-racism education: Theory and practice*. Fernwood Publishing.

Freire, P. (1978). *Pedagogy of the oppressed*. Continuum.

Gay, G. (2010). *Culturally responsive teaching: Theory, research, and practice* (3rd ed.). Teachers College Press.

Hilliard, A. G. (1998). *SBA: The reawakening of the African mind*. Makare Publishing Company.

hooks, b. (2003). *Teaching community: A pedagogy of hope* (1st ed., Vol. 36). Routledge.

Letseka, M. (2000). African voices in education. In P. Higgs, N. C. G. Vakalisa, & N. T. A.-L. T. V. Mda (Eds.), *African philosophy and educational discourse* (pp. 179–193). Juta.

Letseka, M. (2012). In defence of Ubuntu. *Studies in Philosophy and Education, 31*(1), 47–60. https://doi.org/10.1007/s11217-011-9267-2

Mbigi, L. (1997). Images of Ubuntu in global competitiveness. *Flying Springbok, 4*, 31–35.

Mezirow, J. (2000). *Learning as transformation: Critical perspectives on a theory in progress*. Jossey-Bass. https://eric.ed.gov/?id=ED448301

Ngubane, N. I., & Makua, M. (2022). Intersection of Ubuntu pedagogy and social justice: Transforming South African higher education. *Journal of Educational Studies, 45*(3), 245–261. https://doi.org/10.1234/edstudies.v45i3.5678

Ukpokodu, O. N. (2007). Fostering preservice teachers' transformative learning in a social studies methods course: A reflection on transformative pedagogy. *Social Studies Research and Practice, 2*(3), 315–340. https://doi.org/10.1108/SSRP-03-2007-B0002

Ukpokodu, O. N. (2016). *You can't teach us if you don't know us and care about us*. Peter Lang. https://doi.org/10.3726/978-1-4539-1901-9

Venter, E. (2004). The notion of Ubuntu and communication in African educational discourse. *Studies in Philosophy and Education, 23*(2-3), 149–160.

PART THREE

Ubuntu in Context: Botswana and Namibia

"One with Ubuntu is careful to walk in the world as one who recognizes the infinite worth of everyone with whom he or she comes into contact."
–Archbishop Desmond Tutu

Looking Through the Window: Botswana and Namibia

IN THE QUEST TO DEEPLY understand the meaning of Ubuntu in context, I spent several weeks during the summer of 2017 in two countries in Southern Africa, Botswana and Namibia. Both Botswana and Namibia are very culturally and linguistically diverse. I was fully immersed in the culture while in the different countries. I took language classes and learned about the people's history and culture. I also spent time in rural and inner-city schools, working and observing teachers.

Overall, I visited seven schools in the two countries and spoke to several teachers, students, professors, and community members about the idea of Ubuntu. From my conversations with the natives in Botswana, I learned that Ubuntu is one of the five pillars of their country. Ubuntu is incorporated into the elementary schools' grade four social studies curricula. The children are taught how to show respect and care for each other. Spending weeks in Botswana and Namibia has given me an insight into the deep cultural values of the Bantu people.

Botswana

Botswana is a landlocked country, with more than 80% of the land being desert. However, in my eyes, the Kalahari does not look like a desert because the endless thorny trees, shrubs, and red sand contain woodland and other vegetation. There are no rivers or lakes; however, the Okavango Delta is the world's largest inland river delta. Botswana has more than 20 tribes and about 20 languages spoken by the people, but the languages are closely related because of the Bantu root languages from Southern Africa.

The people are warm and welcoming, from the capital of Gaborone to the rural area of Kgomoditshaba, a village in the Kgatleng District of Botswana. When the children or adults see you, they greet you with "*Dumela Rra*," if speaking to a man and "*Dumela Mma*," if speaking to a woman. This is the universal greeting used day and night. A smile always follows the warm greetings. The majority of the people speak Setswana, which has its roots in the Bantu languages. However, the Bantu-speaking people were not the first inhabitants; the San people were the original inhabitants. The San people culture is among the oldest civilizations on Earth.

Living With and Shadowing a Teacher

Living amongst the people in the rural town of Kgomoditshaba, Botswana has taught me a lot about Ubuntu (*Botho*) in action, creativity, and children's natural intelligence. There is a strong sense of community and collective action. The children in the community were caring and creative. They treated each other respectfully, and the older ones cared for the younger ones. The children love each other. It was my first time seeing children as young as 4 years living in boarding schools (hostels). The older children ensure that the younger ones are cared for and ready for school.

One afternoon during lunch, I observed a group of children gathering in numbers around one student. Unfortunately, coming from America, I thought it was a fight, so I investigated. To my surprise, one of the young men in the center had a small parcel of white sugar, and he was sharing it among the students. I asked what was going on, and one of the young girls responded by saying, "He is king. Everyone wants sugar, so he is sharing, teacher." That day, I learned that sugar makes you king, but I saw Ubuntu in action most of all. If one has in abundance, we all have. Sharing is caring! The essence of love and caring was being demonstrated amongst the children.

Namibia

Namibia is a beautiful country with a beautiful landscape and rich culture.

I had the opportunity to speak with members of the *Herero, Oshiwamba, Himba*, and *Khoisan* people. Their diversity is rich, but they share similarities in their cultural practices.

In Namibia, the idea of Ubuntu is entrenched in the cultural values of the society. It was evident in the marketplace and amongst the students in the school. In the market, the vendors were supportive of each other. For instance, if someone purchased an item from one, they were also encouraged to buy it from their neighboring vendor. They also worked as a team in the marketplace. While there, I observed that a group of men bought one cow every week and worked collaboratively in the market to sell the meat and share the profit.

In the schools, the children were very caring and welcoming. As a visitor, I felt welcomed. One morning, I observed a group of boys caring and sharing in the schoolyard. The boys put their money together to buy cooked meat from a vendor and shared it amongst themselves. In the classroom, the students demonstrated caring and loving behaviors with each other. For example, it is a part of school culture for the children to celebrate the success of other students with chants and claps. Whenever a student answered a question, they all chanted and clapped in unison: "You are a superstar, you are a superstar, well done!" The spirit of Ubuntu was evident amongst the students as they celebrated each other's successes. The sense of family and community was important to them all.

Conversations About Discipline With Natives

Visiting and reasoning with teachers and students from seven different schools taught me a lot about the education system in Namibia. When I lectured at the University of Namibia, I had a packed room of teachers, principals, and professors from the university. One of the questions that I was asked was about corporal punishment. In late 2000, corporal punishment was banned in all schools in Namibia, and to date, teachers are struggling with different methods of disciplining the African child. The teachers are seeking solutions to fix the discipline issues in the school.

As a researcher, I understand the issue of discipline is a complex problem; however, I believe that the solution lies within the ancient concept of Ubuntu/Botho. Developing a proactive discipline approach based on the cultural context is essential. No outsiders from Europe and America should teach Africans how to manage their children effectively. To find a solution, we need to look at our indigenous cultural child-rearing practices. We should not use the paradigm forced on us by our invaders—our enemies—to educate our people.

A researcher from the San Project explained that he learned from the San people that one of the reasons they refused to send their children to the government schools is because the schools "beat their children with whips," and they do not hit their children. This was a profound message from the San people, the oldest culture in southern Africa. These ancient people have different ways of disciplining their children, and we need to begin to explore their practice of discipline. We have to explore the idea that every *muntu* (a person) plays a vital in the community.

A *muntu* plays a vital role in developing the collective community in African cosmology. In other words, the muntu plays an essential role because the person shares their center with the family, community, nation, race, and the universe. Therefore, we must design a discipline plan that teaches children that they have their center, but we are inextricably joined to others in our community and our *Kanda* (race). Children must be taught that their actions have a more significant impact on the group. Each person is essential to the group as a whole.

Therefore, we are responsible and mindful of how our behaviors impact the whole. For our children to understand their place in this world, we must explicitly teach them this tenet of *Ubuntu Ngu Muntu Nganga Bantu Zulu*; *Motho ke motho Ka Botha* (*Setsawna*). A person is a person because there are people. They must understand that we are interconnected and interdependent. Our choices of behavior will impact the whole community. At the same time, they must know that their existence is vital to the community. A person cannot exist without the community. The community helps to strengthen and nurture the individual.

Reflection on My Experience in Botswana and Namibia

As an outsider looking in through the "window," I made many observations. I wanted to understand Ubuntu in action, and I witnessed much positive evidence in the schools. However, I saw negative evidence as well. For example, I saw evidence of marginalized children and some teachers operating from deficit minds. I saw evidence of teachers treating children from different ethnic groups unfairly. I believe all teachers can benefit from the Ubuntu pedagogy framework to help counteract the colonizing education practices still being used in schools.

The philosophical and ontological concept informs the Ubuntu pedagogy framework. Ubuntu—an idea that we are human through other people. Ubuntu pedagogy is a revolutionary, counter-hegemonic pedagogical paradigm for restoring teachers' and students' humanity in the practice of education for freedom and genuine love (Freire, 1978). It is grounded in the belief that all students are humans who can excel in their academics if their humanity is placed front and center of their learning (Freire, 1978). Freire also reminds us that "education can be used as an instrument of humanization or dehumanization," and he encouraged us to pick the latter.

Reflection Questions

1. What are your takeaways from this reflection on Ubuntu in Action?
2. How can you demonstrate Ubuntu-oriented style of teaching in your class?

References

Freire, P. (1978). *Pedagogy of the oppressed.* Continuum.

Image 3.1 Visiting schools in Windhoek, Namibia, 2017.

Image 3.2 A Rural primary school in Botswana.

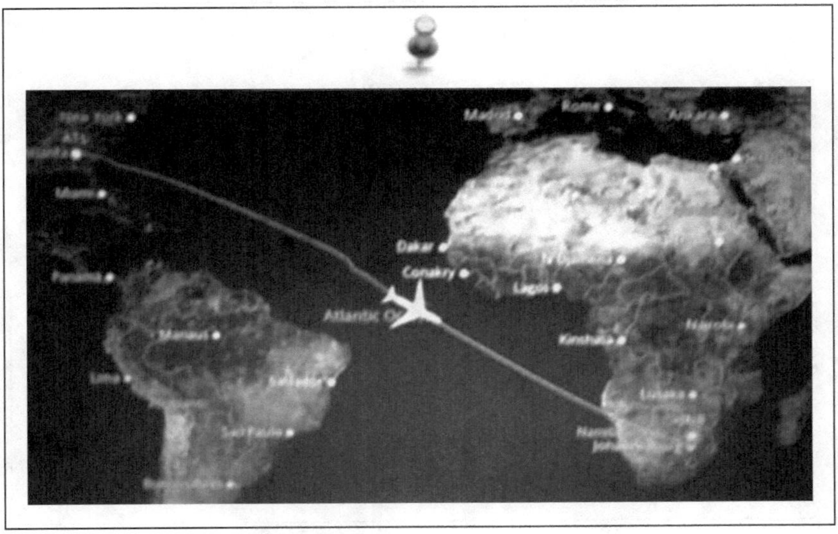

Image 3.3 Journey from USA to Southern Africa.

Image 3.4 Lecturing at the University of Namibia.

Image 3.5 Meeting with government officials to discuss education in Namibia.

PART FOUR

Ubuntu and Discipline

"Punish firmly, chastise soundly,
Then, repression of crime becomes an example.
Punishment except for crime
Turns the complainer into an enemy."
–Ptahhotep, over 5000 years ago (Gunn,1906)

Cultivating Ubuntu Discipline Plan

DISCIPLINE AND ORDER ARE NECESSARY for society. Discipline enables one to choose and persevere with actions, thoughts, and behavior, leading to improvement and success. Discipline is more than following rules and procedures. Positive discipline promotes order in society. Disciplining the mind helps build a strong character in a person. A person who learns and practices self-control of the mind-body-spirit understands how to govern thoughts and emotions. From discipline comes order in society. Order is a clear structure that organizes the habits of the mind. All children need some sense of order to be productive community members. Therefore, teachers must create orderly systems to help children navigate the world.

Order helps cultivate harmonious learning spaces where students can work on relationships with diverse others. Developing an orderly environment starts with self. Educators must be conscious and intentional about their heart, mind, and action habits before building relationships with others.

What Does Creating an Orderly Classroom Environment Look Like?

At the beginning of each school year, I spend the first 6 weeks of school building community by teaching students how to respect each other. I explicitly teach, practice, and reinforce procedures in my class. Teach the students to do what is right and how to care for each other. My class motto is "do what is right because it's the right thing to do, not because someone is watching you." As a teacher, I model what is right and demonstrate caring behaviors inside and outside the classroom. Be very mindful of one's behavior and teach children about self-awareness. Let them know you see them and validate their voices in the school. Be sure to notice when they are doing right and when they are doing wrong. Regardless of the behavior, comment with a firm, gentle tone and state the specific action you want to encourage or discourage. I have learned that before children can be expected to do what is right, they must first be taught what is "right" through the clear establishment and communication of expectations. For example, I have daily routines and rituals the children practice in my classroom. One of the rituals and routines I do in my class is "morning meeting." Morning meeting is an integral part of the daily routines in my classroom. It is used to set the tone of my day and strengthen the social-emotional learning for my students. The morning meeting is strategically designed to ensure students develop healthy habits of mind. During the morning meetings, students learn to respectfully listen and share their feelings with their classmates. The morning meeting ritual builds a sense of community, creates a positive climate for learning, and reinforces academic and social skills. The ritualistic aspect of the morning meeting is based on four components: greeting, sharing, group activity, and message. These four components are the structure I use to teach social-emotional behavior. In the meeting, the children learn about themselves and recognize our interdependence and connectedness to each other. In addition, they understand how their behavior can negatively or positively impact the class. Furthermore, students are taught how to take responsibility for their actions and skills that will help them be productive citizens. I use role-playing and storytelling to model what caring and responsible students do in different situations. I teach lessons of endurance, perseverance, determination, and self-confidence through storytelling and role-play. In addition, the students learn how to set goals and track their academic progress. They also participate in student-led conferences to share what they have learned with their parents or guardians. Social-emotional learning is integrated into every subject area throughout the day. I teach students how to affirm their humanity and have respect for each other. The children are taught how to work cooperatively in groups, problem-solve, and deepen their understanding of the topics. As the students work collaboratively, I model the desirable and undesirable behaviors. I also inform the students of the lesson's goal and set clear expectations. When children are reminded of the academic and social goals in a classroom, it helps them interpret the meaning of what they are doing and grow academically and socially as young scholars.

I have worked in urban schools with culturally and linguistically diverse students for most of my teaching career. Over the years, I have learned that children are not born with the understanding of how to resolve conflicts; they must be taught. Nevertheless, conflicts and confrontation are part of their growing and learning environment. Therefore, I teach students problem-solving strategies in my class by creating the Ubuntu Reflective Corner. The Ubuntu Reflective Corner is placed in the classroom so children can learn techniques and tools to help them regulate conflict within themselves or with others. The children use a variety of strategies to calm themselves and reflect on their behavior to move from confrontation to conciliation.

The tools used to calm the children include squeeze balls, music, journaling, and reflective thinking sheets, which they use to meditate on their feelings.

The Ubuntu reflective corner is a self-directed place where children can reflect and reset before rejoining the class community. Self-reflection helps students regulate their emotions before joining the community.

Furthermore, I also incorporate best practices such as brain energizer activities, music, and movements between subject matters to build a strong classroom community. Brain energizers are physical activity breaks during class time, which help children relax and stimulate the brain to remain engaged during teaching and learning. Research shows that physical movement increases blood flow, bringing more oxygen to the brain and improving mental concentration (Jensen, 2000). The classroom environment should be orderly, allowing children to move around and take charge of their learning. For example, I provide clear expectations to cultivate self-directed learners using the CHAMPS acronym for Conversation, Help, Activity, Movement, Participation, and Success (Sprick, 2009).

The CHAMPS acronym is a proactive classroom management system that helps to engage and motivate students toward positive behaviors. There are several questions that an instructor using CHAMPS thinks about before assigning students to complete a task. For instance, an instructor may ask and answer questions such as: **Conversation:** Can students converse during this activity? About what? With whom? For how long? **Help**: How do students get your attention for help? How do students get questions answered? What should they do while they wait for you? **Activity**: What is the expected product of this activity? What is the task or objective? **Movement**: For what reasons can students get out of their seats during this activity? Do they need permission to do so? **Participation**: What behaviors show whether students are participating or not? **Success**: Are the expectations clear? Are the students more motivated to learn? Are they more engaged in the teaching and learning processes (Sprick, 2009)?

Using the CHAMPS acronym in the class provides clear directions for the students and explicit instructions regarding their expectations. When expectations are clear, students become more engaged and develop the skills to become self-directed learners within the community context.

How to Utilize the Ubuntu Teaching Framework

The Ubuntu pedagogy framework is a structure that educators can utilize to create a positive discipline plan for their students. Ubuntu pedagogy states that educators must first understand themselves. Understanding ourselves requires unpacking our personal biases, recognizing our cultural identities, and being aware of any shortcomings before we start working with children. In addition, understanding the self helps us build caring relationships with others.

Building relationships with students is a fundamental component of academic success. When students feel cared for by their teachers, they become motivated and work diligently. The classroom is a community, and it is essential, as the class leaders, to unify the students, encouraging them to work together. The teacher's responsibility is to help students understand that they are interdependent and their actions can positively or negatively impact others. Building a strong class community is essential to nurture the children's minds and help them develop a growth mindset. When children are taught to persevere through challenges, they are more likely to build resilience. Research has shown that children with a growth mindset are better equipped to continue striving for success despite challenges (Dweck, 2015).

Additionally, teaching from a position of love and care is essential to students' academic and social development. It is also important to teach children to care for and recognize when others care for and love them. Using positive language for guidance helps children develop courage and confidently tackle their academic work (Noddings, 2002). When children are confident in their abilities, both the children and the teacher enjoy the students' success in school. Educators should also utilize evidence-based practices to ensure they are meeting the diverse needs of all their students. To meet students' diverse needs, one has to study the students and make conscientious, explicit decisions while using evidence from multiple sources of data to help monitor students' progress so that they can grow academically.

Here are some examples of an African-centered school discipline plan.

Ubuntu Discipline Framework

- Understanding of self
- Building authentic relationships
- Unifying the class to work together
- Nurturing the minds of the children
- Teaching from a position of love and care, and
- Utilizing evidence-based practices to meet the diverse needs of the students

Discipline Policy

Ubuntu -"I am because we are."
We do not practice corporal punishment.
We use a proactive approach to correct behaviors.
We use misbehavior as an opportunity to teach.

Core Values

Teamwork

- By emphasizing teamwork, we cultivate a shared sense of purpose among teachers, parents, and students.
- We actively encourage the involvement of volunteers and the broader community.
- We promote and sustain a culture of shared leadership and collective responsibility.

Prioritizing Student Success

- We believe that all children can focus on building upon their strengths.
- We inspire and challenge all students to achieve success.
- We create an environment where students are empowered, giving them ownership and a voice.

A Strong Instructional Program Is Rooted in Fostering an Ethic of Care Through Cultural Values

Our curriculum integrates the ethics of care by drawing upon the rich African value systems of Ubuntu philosophy, the seven principles of MAAT, and the NGUZO SABA (The Seven Principles of Kwanzaa). These cultural frameworks emphasize:

Ubuntu Philosophy

- Interconnectedness and shared humanity
- "I am because we are."
- Compassion and mutual caring

Seven Principles of MAAT

1. Truth
2. Justice
3. Harmony
4. Balance
5. Order
6. Reciprocity
7. Propriety

NGUZO SABA (Seven Principles of Kwanzaa)

1. Umoja (Unity)
2. Kujichagulia (Self-Determination)
3. Ujima (Collective Work and Responsibility)
4. Ujamaa (Cooperative Economics)

5. Nia (Purpose)
6. Kuumba (Creativity)
7. Imani (Faith)

By integrating these principles through traditional and innovative teaching methods, our curriculum motivates and accommodates our students' individual needs and interests and fosters an ethic of care. This culturally grounded approach enables students to excel academically while being recognized and celebrated for their achievements, enhancing their overall development.

We Are Lifelong Learners

- Staff and students are actively engaged and enthusiastic about learning.
- We respect and support each other's passions.
- We practice reflective thinking with a purposeful intent to grow and deepen our understanding of authentic African culture.

Safe and Happy School Environment

We cultivate a welcoming, nurturing, and safe environment.

- Life skills are modeled, taught, and reinforced throughout the school.
- Expectations are consistent.
- Relationships are founded on good communication, trust, and mutual respect among staff, students, parents, and community members.
- We take pride in our work! We are committed, energetic, and optimistic about nurturing future Black leaders.

Steps to a Proactive and Positive Discipline Plan

- Develop a deep understanding of your students.
- Communicate effectively and teach classroom expectations.
- Collaboratively establish classroom norms, whether in person or virtually.
- Exemplify kind, supportive, and respectful behavior.
- Regularly review classroom norms and expectations.
- Address and redirect student behavior with positive language.

- Implement a system to recognize and celebrate student effort and growth.
- Utilize nonverbal signals for support, recognition, or redirection.
- Frequently check in with students and offer gestures of support.

Reflection Questions

1. How do you establish an environment conducive to student success?
2. What strategies do you employ to ensure students achieve success?
3. What is your discipline plan for both virtual and face-to-face classes?
4. How do you foster strong relationships with your students?
5. What comprehensive discipline plan do you implement?

References

Dweck, C. S. (2015). Carol Dweck revisits the "growth mindset." *Education Week, 35*(5), 20–24.

Jensen, E. (2000). Moving with the brain in mind. *Educational Leadership, 58*(3), 34–37.

Gunn, B. G. (Trans.). (1906). *The instruction of Ptah-Hotep and the instruction of Ke'Gemni: The oldest books in the world.* Project Gutenberg. https://www.gutenberg.org/files/30508/30508-h/30508-h.htm

Noddings, N. (2002). *Starting at home: Caring and social policy.* University of California Press.

Sprick, R. S. (2009). *CHAMPS: A proactive and positive approach to classroom management* (2nd ed.). Pacific Northwest Publishing.

PART FIVE

Ubuntu in Action

"Only when culturally competent teaching is routinely available will culturally different students have a chance to reach their full potentials."
–Jean Moule

Ubuntu Competence and Discipline

As an educator, having confidence in yourself and your abilities is important. A teacher with little confidence is not attractive to students. As a result, they often get mistreated, ridiculed, and disrespected by students. Therefore, teachers should consistently demonstrate confidence in what they know or don't know. If you don't know something, confidently admit it and assure the students you will do your best to find out.

If a student rudely interrupts, as they will do sometimes, confidently say to them, "Please allow me to do my job! Thank you!" When a teacher is confident in their abilities, the students appear more confident and will listen and follow the teacher.

The Conceptual Framework for Cultivating Ubuntu Competence

Figure 5.1: Conceptual Framework, Blackwood (2018)

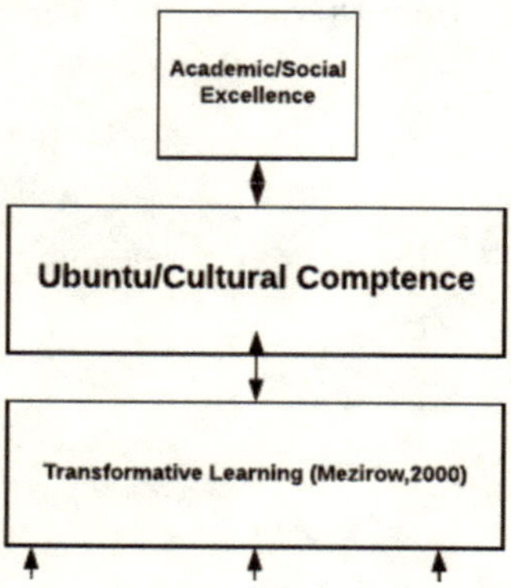

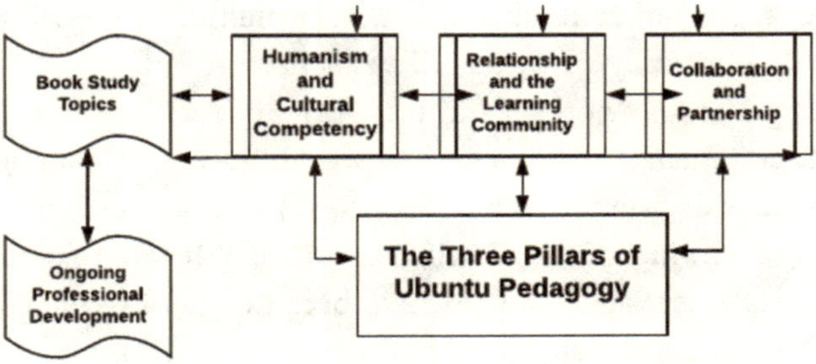

Cultural Competence

Cultural competence is a set of attitudes, behaviors, actions, knowledge, skills, and abilities to work and respond more effectively in cross-cultural contexts (Gay, 2010). It entails mastering complex self-awareness, accepting differences, and adapting skills to changing cultural needs and demands (Moule, 2005, p. 27).

Ukpokodu (2016) defined cultural competence as the "will and ability to extend oneself, form authentic relationships, understand, communicate, and effectively interact with diverse others" (p. 43). Culturally competent teachers are deeply knowledgeable about using the students' culture as a vehicle to engage them in pedagogical content. Furthermore, Ukpokodu (2016) posited that teachers could move beyond cultural competence and reach Ubuntu competence when they recognize their humanity and willingness to accept, affirm, and dignify others.

Ubuntu Competence

According to Ukpokodu (2016), Ubuntu competence is the ability of an educator to fully live their humanity by being deeply knowledgeable that their society is intricately intertwined with the humanity of others. Ubuntu competence is an ongoing developmental process requiring teachers to know themselves and be mindful and intentional about how they interact with diverse others. When building genuine relationships with students, it is important to be knowledgeable about self and to affirm the humanity of others. To affirm the humanity of others, teachers need to understand how to show love, empathy, kindness, reciprocity, and humility.

This deeper level of cultural competence is multidimensional. It requires teachers to be critically conscious of who they are and intentionally take the time to get to know others and their culture. Sociocultural researchers support the argument that teachers must possess the critical consciousness to help them make decisions that will impact, validate, and empower students in a learning environment (Gay, 2010; Ukpokodu, 2016). Developing cultural competence is essential for all teachers because, in our changing world, educators must be culturally competent to teach healing, peace, love, and social justice in a democratic society.

Cultivating one's humanity is anchored in transformative learning—a learning process in which a person experiences a profound, structural shift in consciousness that changes their ways of being in the world. Book studies are a great way to cultivate and transform teachers' minds. Therefore, I would recommend the book *You Can't Teach Us if You Don't Know Us and Care About Us: Becoming an Ubuntu, Responsive and Responsible Urban Teacher* by Omiunota Nelly Ukpokodu. The book addresses the needs of diverse urban students for a new kind of teacher, classroom learning context, curriculum, and pedagogy to learn, perform, and achieve effectively. Emphasis is placed on Ubuntu pedagogy as a model to emulate, anchored on five ethical dimensions: humanism and Ubuntu competence, relationship and learning community, humanism in the curriculum, pedagogical and instructional excellence, and collaboration and partnership. It is particularly valuable for teachers to learn to cultivate the spirit of Ubuntu that undergirds their ability to be humane, responsive, and social.

To further support teachers' understanding of cultivating Ubuntu competence and transforming their mindset, they all participate in a book club. The three pillars of Ubuntu pedagogy are humanism and competency, relationship and learning community, collaboration and partnership, and transformative learning.

Cultural Competence Versus Ubuntu Competence

A teacher who works with a diverse group of students must always seek to understand the students' cultural norms and know how to use the information in a cross-cultural context to keep the students engaged in learning the content being taught. A culturally competent teacher always seeks ways to make lessons meaningful and relevant to the students' interests or cultures. A culturally competent teacher knows how to keep the students engaged and support compliance and academic achievement.

An Ubuntu-responsive educator thinks about the students in all aspects, the classroom environment's structure and the lesson delivery to students. The students are placed at the center of learning. Also, they are actively aware and take ownership of their learning. An Ubuntu-responsive teacher connects with the students' spirits when teaching. When a teacher connects deeply to the essence of their students, Dr. Asa Hilliard (1998) refers to this as a "spiritual dance" in the book *SBA*. When there is order and balance in the classroom, it manifests in the actions and words of the students. The students are more likely to be self-directed and motivated to do their best daily. There is also a strong sense of community, and collaboration takes place among the students. The spirit of "brother's keeper" is evident in the interaction of the students. They work collaboratively to make sure their fellow students are safe and learning.

An Ubuntu educator is a deep thinker. When designing a learning space, the children are at the center of the decision-making process. Some of the critical questions to think about are:

- What kind of learners do we have?
- What kind of learners do we want to develop?
- What should they know?
- How do we achieve our goal?

In a student-centered learning environment, the children are at the center of the decision-making process. Therefore, the teacher is intentional about the plans for the children's success.

Learning Environment

An Ubuntu-competent teacher creates a learning environment of order, balance, and harmony. This is evident in the teacher's tone and the way children interact with each other as soon as they enter the space.

Teacher Text and Tone

As educators, we must create learning spaces that are kind and loving. It is imperative to teach children how to love each other. They must demonstrate love for the children and care about their well-being. This should be a semi-biotic relationship. The educator must explicitly teach the child how to show love and respect for all. The teacher may use stories, movies, and the actions of others to teach examples and nonexamples of love. A teacher must model the desirable behaviors at all times.

Teach the children how to be kind. Kindness is a fundamental moral value that should be taught to children. The teachers should also demonstrate kindness in action and words. Also, be intentional about pointing out kind deeds in stories and real life. For example, a teacher can write a note to the class to tell them how they love them.

Additionally, take every opportunity to have children show gratitude to their peers and others. For instance, the child can make teacher appreciation day cards or birthday cards or write kind notes and share them with students and staff on the campus. The child can write a note to an elder in the community thanking them for something they did. Although teaching kindness is not reserved for younger children, it should also be demonstrated at the secondary level. A teacher can show kindness by speaking respectfully, listening deeply to students, and suspending judgment. An Ubuntu-competent teacher is aware of his or her hidden biases and should take action so that they do not affect their relationship with others.

Ubuntu in Action

The core elements of Ubuntu are humanity, connectedness, community, harmony, interdependence, relationship, and respect. Ubuntu competence is a multidimensional and ongoing developmental process requiring educators to be cognizant of building harmonious relationships with diverse others. Educators must cultivate Ubuntu competence that involves habits of heart, habits of the mind, and habits of action to build relationships with diverse others.

Voices From Teachers in the Field

Guiding Question: How do you build relationships with your students?

I interviewed the schoolteachers, who explained how relationships matter and a caring class culture could help children succeed in school.

Middle School Teachers

For 10 years, Ms. McLean (pseudonym), a veteran middle school teacher, stated that "when teachers build genuine relationships with the students, it helps to establish trust and open communication." She explained that her classroom operates similarly to a family.

The students feel a sense of belonging because they treat each other like family. The democratic process also guides her classroom, making decisions based on group consensus. For example, Ms. McLean spoke about using the knowledge of a *Kgotla* (a town meeting) she learned while studying in Botswana to structure her daily class meetings. In a *Kgotla* (COAT-la), the elders and the community members discuss issues using a democratic process. The Chief facilitates the discussion, but each member of the town has a voice. Likewise, the daily class meetings are designed for the teachers and the students to converse about a topic and learn problem-solving skills.

Mr. Murray (pseudonym), a veteran teacher for 21 years in urban schools, stated that to build relationships with the students and families, it is crucial that "you show them that you care and listen to them." Ms. Daniels (pseudonym), an urban teacher for 13 years, also stated that it is important to establish "trust with the students and mean what you say and do what you say." When students do not trust a teacher, getting them to work for them is hard. Also, she stated that teachers must talk to students like they are human and share relatable life stories with the students. Furthermore, it is essential for teachers to be aware of their biases, be self-reflective, and explicitly teach students how to manage their emotions.

Ms. Daniels (pseudonym) also shared that to be successful in an "urban school, it is important to be self-aware and work daily to make sure biases do not interfere with learning."

How to Cultivate Habits of Mind and Heart?

Habits of the Mind

Habits of mind refer to one's ability to be genuinely knowledgeable about oneself as a human being, a cultural being, and a member of the global society—the ability to recognize our interdependence and connectedness to other humans. When we understand this on a molecular level, we become more mindful of how we treat others who don't look like us, speak like us, or share the same cultural backgrounds. We must learn to recognize that we are humans and that we are unique in how we talk, look, and behave. We must understand that although we do things differently, we are still humans with feelings. We must be mindful of how we treat each other because our negative or positive actions greatly impact others. We have to learn to love ourselves first to extend ourselves to others. When we understand how we are and are comfortable with ourselves, we are at the stage to love and care for diverse others.

Habits of mind are how to think through a problematic situation and find the best solution to address the nature of the problem. For example, if a student encounters a complex problem, ask self-questions such as:

What is the most intelligent thing I can do right now?

- What can I learn from this?
- What are my resources?
- How can I draw on my past successes with problems like this?
- What do I already know about the problem?
- What resources do I have available or need to generate?
- How can I approach this problem flexibly?
- How might I look at the situation in another way?
- How can I draw upon my repertoire of problem-solving strategies? How can I look at this problem from a fresh perspective?
- How does this problem affect others?
- How can we solve it together?
- What can I learn from others to help me become a better problem solver?

These are some questions one can explore and store in the toolbox to have the skill set to navigate difficult situations. Educators hold one of the noblest roles in cultivating young minds. To fulfill this duty, we must continually ensure our minds are in the right place. This involves doing inner work and regularly reflecting on our actions and thoughts. Teaching demands daily engagement in deep self-reflection. Ubuntu-responsive educators should not wait for an administrator or mentor to tell them to reflect; it should be part of their daily practice as educators. Ubuntu-competent educators are self-aware, build authentic relationships, respect themselves, and dignify others. Most of all, teachers with Ubuntu competence work to humanize and not dehumanize others.

Habits of the Heart

Habits of the heart involve freely expressing compassion, empathy, kindness, reciprocity, dignity, and humility. They also foster harmonious coexistence within our human community and nurture our sense of justice, equity, and humanity.

The habit of action speaks to our ability to act in ways that let us embrace, value, affirm and dignify the humanity of others, advocate, and disrupt conditions that dehumanize others (Ukpokodu, 2016). Educators of the 21st century and beyond must develop critical consciousness. To do so, they must understand their cultural selves and recognize that their existence is not separate from anyone else's. They must also cultivate harmonious relationships with others and speak in ways that dignify humanity.

Once teachers are grounded in an understanding of self, they can better develop orderly and safe environments where students feel comfortable taking risks and participating in behaviors that humanize instead of dehumanizing each other.

Ms. Stanley's Story

Teachers who nurture the heart's habits develop a keen sense of justice and equity towards humanity. When teachers cultivate habits of heart, it is evident in their practice.

For example, meet *Profile of Ms. Stanley*

- Veteran Teacher (20 years of teaching)
- Public School

Ms. Stanley is a passionate master teacher. I have known her for 9 years. She is also a caring teacher who takes the time to get to know her students. During the first 21 days of school, Ms. Stanley incorporated several community-building activities in her class. During a classroom observation, I noticed that Ms. Stanley speaks to the children in a clear and calm voice while providing explicit directions to the students about the activities for the morning meeting. As previously stated, morning meeting is the time of the day when the students interact and build relationships with each other. In an interview, Ms. Stanley candidly spoke about how she builds relationships with her students. She stated she does "not have a problem building relationships with my students."

I invest in my students! "I take a lot of time to build relationships with my children, and we have a lot of heart-to-heart conversations. I'm not afraid to share parts of my life with them." As a result, they understand that they are not alone in what they are going through. "I encourage my students to speak often about their thoughts and feelings, fostering regular self-expression. We celebrate even the smallest successes together." For instance, if their grade moves from an F to a D, that's still a celebration because I see [they] are trying [their] best. I celebrate their small successes along the way. That's just as important as getting an 'A' in my class. I tell my kids I love them every day! Some of them are quite shy about it at the beginning of the year, but towards the middle of the year, when I say I love you, they immediately say I love you, too. My students like hugs, and by mid-year, everybody gets a hug when they come in and when they leave my class daily."

Getting to know her students is paramount. Ms. Stanley has a personal relationship with all her students. She takes the time to learn about them on both a personal and an academic level. She is very intentional about how she interacts with her students. For example, she tells the students that she is biracial, her mother is white, and her father is Black. She uses her cultural identity to teach lessons of tolerance and social justice in the class. She also tells her students that she loves them. Throughout the day, Ms. Stanley makes it a priority to do a check-in meeting with her students. After lunchtime, she conducts a brief check-in meeting with her students before beginning with academic content. The check-in meeting is another ongoing way for her to build relationships with her students. She stated that the check-in meetings allow her students to talk and say what's on their minds because they do not have enough time to talk at lunch. Furthermore, Ms. Stanley goes above and beyond to develop family partnerships. Although she reported that getting her students' parents to attend scheduled parent conferences is challenging, she finds many ways to connect with parents. For example, sometimes she conducts phone conferences and home visits. She has a reputation for showing up at her students' homes to provide support and address academic concerns.

One day, she received the unfortunate news that one of her student's sisters had died. Ms. Stanley immediately reached out to the family to provide support, and when the child was ready to return to school, she prepared the class to welcome the student back and help her readjust to school life. Ms. Stanley is an Ubuntu-responsive educator because she knows how to show love, build authentic relationships, and touch the humanity in others.

Habits of Action

Educators of the 21st century and beyond must develop their critical consciousness by understanding their cultural selves and recognizing that their existence is not separate from anyone else's. Therefore, we must cultivate harmonious relationships with others and speak in ways that dignify humanity. Ms. Stanley's story shows evidence of Ubuntu's competence in how she humanizes her students. As an Ubuntu-responsive educator, Ms. Stanley is proactive in her approaches to teaching the class. She integrates social-emotional learning in the content area. She is intentional about knowing how her students feel and think before teaching the content. She knows how to connect to the hearts and minds of the students through her actions.

Ubuntu-responsive teachers must be mindful of their seen and unseen behaviors. Children watch our actions on how we respond to people or situations. Children pay close attention to our verbal and nonverbal cues. The students listen carefully to our words and how we respond to challenges.

Ubuntu-responsive educators are skilled in facilitating difficult conversations with students without biases. They know how to be objective and help their students think critically about the situation. As educators, we must create empowering learning spaces and build a strong sense of community. It is possible, but we first have to understand ourselves, develop authentic relationships with others, and consciously take action to help create an atmosphere where learners can thrive emotionally and academically.

Reflection Questions

1. How can you create a welcoming learning environment?
2. What changes can you make in your teaching practice?
3. What does it mean to listen deeply and withhold judgment?

References

Blackwood, A. (2018). *Transformative learning: Improving teachers' cultural competencies through knowledge and practice of Ubuntu pedagogy* [Doctoral dissertation, College of Education and Human Performance]. http://purl.fcla.edu/fcla/etd/CFE0007157

Gay, G. (2010). *Culturally responsive teaching: Theory, research, and practice* (3rd ed.). Teachers College Press.

Hilliard, A. G. (1998). *SBA: The reawakening of the African mind*. Makare Publishing Company.

Mezirow, J. (2000a). *Learning as transformation: Critical perspectives on a theory in progress*. Jossey-Bass. https://eric.ed.gov/?id=ED448301

Mezirow, J. (2000b). Learning to think like an adult: Core concepts of transformation theory. In J. Mezirow & Associates (Eds.), *Learning as transformation: Critical perspectives on a theory in progress* (pp. 3–34). Jossey-Bass. https://eric.ed.gov/?id=ED448301

Moule, J. (2012). *Cultural competence: A primer for educators* (2nd ed.). Wadsworth, Cengage Learning.

Ukpokodu, O. N. (2016). *You can't teach us if you don't know us and care about us*. Peter Lang Verlag. https://doi.org/10.3726/978-1-4539-1901-9

PART SIX

We Teach Who We Are

A person who knows
And knows not that they know
Is asleep – awaken them
A person who knows
And knows that they know
Is wise – follow them
All of these persons reside in you.
Know Thy Self
And to Maat be true
–Anthony T. Browder

Author's Positionality

My experience is wrapped up in my identity as a Black woman, a second-generation immigrant from Jamaica who traced her roots to Africa and values the wisdom of my African ancestors. My grandmother, grandfather, mother, and community raised me. They were my first teachers. My grandmother taught me how to cook and shared her in-depth knowledge of nature and medicinal plants. On the other hand, my grandfather taught me to read and write and cultivate a garden.

My mother taught me how to love unconditionally and the science of baking. For the first 10 years of my life, I grew up in a small farming community in Jamaica. The community was my extended family. I learned how to pool our resources and share. All these experiences made me who I am today. Reflecting, I realized that family and community were important in my development. I worked hard to create humanizing learning spaces as a classroom teacher. I ensured that all students felt valued as members of the class community. It did not matter if I taught online or face to face. Instead, I spent time building relationships with and getting to know them through engaging in activities and dialogue. As a result, the students feel safe in my classes, and all voices matter. In addition, the students know and feel safe sharing life's challenges that might impact their learning with me. My goal is always to create a humanizing learning space for all students. From a humanized environment, equity-minded practice and inclusion flow naturally. While I cannot fix all the social problems, I can show them that I care and see their humanity. I genuinely believe that as an educator, I must make sure that my students feel safe and happy when they are around me. Teaching is more than a job. Teachers are placed in a position of power and are the masters of the community of children. Teachers are in the position to either uplift or destroy the impressionable minds of the children. Teachers can be a significant influence on the minds of the students. They are sometimes seen in a godlike position.

Children Mirror Teachers' Behavior

Profile: Mrs. Green

Public School Teacher With 18 Years' Experience Teaching Kindergarten

I worked with a fantastic kindergarten teacher for over 10 years. She is masterful at teaching kindergarten. Everything about her class is orderly. The little 5-year-old children emulate her. She is very loving and caring to the children. The students are disciplined because she spends the first 21 days of school teaching them clear expectations. She teaches them to think critically and solve problems at an early age.

Mrs. Green is a poised and respectful teacher, and when you see her students, they demonstrate the same behavior. In an interview, she explains her teaching philosophy by stating that she believes in showing the children love. Therefore, she creates a fun-loving, safe, and caring class community for all the children, who learn early to respect themselves and others.

Ms. York's Teaching Philosophy

Profile: Ms. York

Master Educator With Over 30 Years' Experience in Education (Public and Private Schools and Higher Education)

Ms. York is a master teacher who uses nature, life, and culture to cultivate a strong classroom community. Here is her view on creating humanism in the classroom:

> Learning is a natural process. All living things learn and adapt to new information. I feel my job as an educator is much more than just teaching the youths new information. It's to inspire, cultivate, empower and guide. Every child has unique interests and talents. They are also filled with cultural and social affiliations critical to their positive development. As educators, we are the foundation and catalyst for the holistic development of our students. Our impression of these young minds reaches further than reading, mathematics, and sciences. It's important that we assess and observe each student's individual needs, socially, culturally, educationally, and emotionally, and assist them in exploring the vast opportunities of this world and where they fit in. Self-esteem and internal and cultural values are keys to nurturing the more profound meaning in their lives and how they will contribute to our larger society.

When an educator takes the time to get to know and truly appreciate the gifts each child brings to the class, this validation builds a strong foundation for inspiring and cultivating the inner genius within each child and increases their desire to become successful. With this attribute, each student is equipped with the internal drive and confidence to succeed in anything they choose to do in the future. Building self-aware and self-confident students who are encouraged to excel in academics and their character, style, cultural expression, and other critical areas will ensure that each child is prepared to do their best within our global society.

These teachers are examples of Ubuntu-responsive educators. Ubuntu-responsive educators acknowledge their own humanity and see the humanity in others. They validate and affirm the students. Compassion is their core, teaching from a position of love and care. It is evident in how they speak to children and the pedagogical moves in the class. These teachers set high expectations for themselves and their students. They are accountable for the students' overall social-emotional and academic learning. Ubuntu-responsive educators use every opportunity to integrate moral values into their curriculum. Character development is not taught in isolation; it is integrated into the subject area. For example, if the students read a novel, the Ubuntu-responsive educator would identify standards or nonexamples of love, respect, honesty, and responsibility. They are intentional about developing the character of the child. An Ubuntu-responsive educator is skilled in identifying humanism in the curriculum.

Humanism in Curriculum

A curriculum is a guide or a roadmap to help one master the content area. The etymology of the word curriculum comes from the Latin root "*currere*," which means to run a course. A curriculum is designed to program the mind with various intentional steps. There are three major types of curricula: implicit, hidden, and explicit.

An *implicit curriculum* consists of lessons derived from the school's culture and the unintended behaviors, attitudes, and expectations within that culture. *Hidden curricula* carry subliminal messages that aren't explicitly planned, and instructors often aren't aware of their long-term impact on students. Institutions and corporations with hidden agendas often influence these curricula.

An *explicit curriculum* covers subject areas that align with the school's core mission. It goes beyond basic knowledge and skills, aiming for deeper learning that encourages critical thinking. There is no one-size-fits-all curriculum; it must be tailored to the needs of families and communities. A curriculum is pointless if it does not serve the people's needs.

Ubuntu-responsive educators are the masters of the curriculum. They are intentional about building positive relationships with their students. They seek out humanism in the curriculum and ensure that the students master the content and the context in which the information is presented. These educators ensure that the student's culture is incorporated into their work. They see value in the student's culture and bring it to the forefront of learning.

Explore the questions below:

1. Who am I?
2. What is your purpose?
3. What is your passion?
4. What is your teaching philosophy?
5. Why do you want to teach?
6. How do you feel about children?
7. Who inspired you on your educational journey?
8. Describe an amazing teacher you had during your schooling.
9. What is your teaching philosophy?

How to Write a Teaching Philosophy

Your teaching philosophy is a self-reflective statement of your beliefs about teaching and learning. The statement should convey your core values about being what it means to be an effective teacher in the context of your discipline. It is important to explain your core value using specific, concrete examples of what the teacher and learners will do to achieve those goals. Importantly, your teaching philosophy statement also explains why you choose these options.

Guiding questions to think about as you write your philosophy of teaching.

- What knowledge, skills, and attitudes are important for student success in your discipline?
- What are you preparing students for?
- What are key challenges in the teaching-learning process?
- What teaching methods do you use?
- How do these methods contribute to your goals for students?
- Why are these methods appropriate for use in your discipline?
- How do I know when I am effectively teaching?
- What beliefs, theories, and methods mark my successful teaching?
- What types of outcomes do I want for my students?
- How do I develop and maintain positive relationships with students?
- How do I collaborate with others?
- How do I create a supportive learning environment?
- What approach or strategy has worked exceptionally well in my discipline?
- What are my most important learning goals?
- How have/can I make a difference in the lives of your students?

How to Write a Teaching Philosophy Statement

Step 1: Reflect on Your Beliefs and Values

- Identify your core values about teaching and learning.
- Consider the knowledge, skills, and attitudes important for student success in your discipline.

- Think about what you are preparing students for and the key challenges in the teaching-learning process.

Step 2: Answer Guiding Questions

Reflect on the following questions to articulate your beliefs and methods.

- What teaching methods do you use, and why are they appropriate for your discipline?
- How do these methods contribute to your goals for students?
- How do you know when you are effectively teaching?
- What outcomes do you want for your students?
- How do you develop and maintain positive relationships with students?
- How do you collaborate with others?
- How do you create a supportive learning environment?
- What strategies have worked exceptionally well in your discipline?
- What are your most important learning goals?
- How have you made a difference in the lives of your students?

Step 3: Write a Draft

- Begin with an introduction that outlines your core beliefs about teaching and learning.
- Provide specific examples of teaching methods and strategies you use.
- Explain how these methods achieve your teaching goals.
- Discuss how you assess effective teaching and student success.
- Highlight how you build relationships and create a positive learning environment.
- Conclude with your vision for the future and your ongoing commitment to student success.

Step 4: Revise and Refine

- Review your draft for clarity and coherence.
- Ensure your statement is concise and free of jargon.
- Seek feedback from colleagues or mentors.
- Make necessary revisions to strengthen your statement.

Step 5: Finalize Your Statement

- Ensure your statement is well-organized and polished.
- Keep the length appropriate (typically 1 to 2 pages).
- Include specific, concrete examples to illustrate your points.
- Reflect on your teaching philosophy periodically and update it as needed.

Following these steps can create a comprehensive and reflective teaching philosophy statement that clearly conveys your approach to education (Center for Excellence in Learning and Teaching, n.d.). Do not proceed to the next section until you have completed your teaching philosophy.

My Philosophy of Teaching

"He who does not know can know from learning."
–African Proverb

Teaching is my passion. I have been honing my skills for over 20 years in urban P-12 schools. I am always on the quest to find new and innovative ways of imparting knowledge to the students and teachers I work with. Care and compassion for all humanity are core values that I incorporate into my life. Thus, creating learning spaces that are caring and loving is fundamental to my teaching identity. A few years ago, I was told by a professor who studied in South Africa that I teach in the spirit of "Ubuntu." Ubuntu is a word from the Bantu languages in Southern Africa that means humanness or the essence of being human.

My philosophy of how I approach teaching and learning is grounded in the concept of Ubuntu. Ubuntu pedagogy is a holistic framework that is supported by research. Ubuntu is an all-inclusive worldview that considers values shared across cultures, encompassing care, compassion, empathy, honesty, hospitality, respect, and tolerance. Ukpokodu (2016) explains that Ubuntu pedagogy is a humanistic approach to engaging and empowering students' active learning. It is grounded in the belief that all students can excel academically if their humanity is placed front and center of their learning. It is from a humanistic viewpoint that I approach teaching and learning.

As an educator, one of my goals is to create learning spaces that allow all learners to feel dignified as human beings. The concept of Ubuntu is transformative because it constantly reminds us that we are a part of an interdependent and interconnected relationship. Ubuntu pedagogy elevates the notion of being a responsive and socially just teacher as it captures the importance of understanding oneself and how to build relationships with others.

The six components of Ubuntu pedagogy that serve as the guiding principles of how I approach teaching and learning are:

- Understanding of self
- Building relationships with others
- Unifying the community
- Nurturing the habits of mind and heart
- Teaching from a position of love and care, and
- Utilizing evidence-based practices to meet the diverse needs of all learners

Incorporating the Ubuntu-oriented teaching style as part of my teaching identity has helped to elevate my understanding of culturally responsive teaching and the notion of teaching for social justice. The underpinnings of the Ubuntu concept are that we are humans, and it is essential that we act in ways that embrace, value, and dignify the humanity of others. Paulo Freire writes that education can act as an instrument of "humanization and dehumanization" and asks that we choose the former. As a student of Freire and a transformative educator, my goal is to educate in a way that disrupts systemic inequities, injustice, and systems that dehumanize people. I believe that students can only cultivate complex skills and competencies in humane and dialogical learning spaces and with educators who value humanity.

Therefore, as an educator, I strive to provide learning spaces that validate, affirm, and dignify all learners.

Conceptual Framework Reflection Questions

1. What is your teaching philosophy? Explain it in three sentences or less. ***Sample Answer:*** *My teaching philosophy is grounded in the principles of*

Ubuntu, emphasizing community, connection, and equity. I believe in creating an inclusive and supportive learning environment where students feel valued and empowered to succeed. My approach centers on culturally responsive teaching, integrating students' backgrounds and experiences into the learning process to make it relevant and meaningful.

2. How do you ensure students follow the rules and meet expectations?
3. What advice would you give to a new teacher?
4. How do you demonstrate that you care about your students?

References

Browder, A. T. (1992). *Nile Valley contributions to civilization (Exploding the myths, Vol. 1)*. Institute of Karmic Guidance.

Center for Excellence in Learning and Teaching. (n.d.). *Writing a teaching philosophy statement*. Iowa State University. https://www.celt.iastate.edu/instructional-strategies/document-your-teaching/writing-a-teaching-philosophy-statement/

Ukpokodu, O. N. (2016). *You can't teach us if you don't know us and care about us*. Peter Lang Verlag. https://doi.org/10.3726/978-1-4539-1901-9

Tulley, M., & Chiu, L. H. (1998). Children's perceptions of the effectiveness of classroom discipline techniques. *Journal of Instructional Psychology, 25*, 189–197.

Weinstein C., Tomlinson-Clarke S., & Curran, M. (2004). Toward a conception of culturally responsive classroom management. *Journal of Teacher Education, 55*(1), 25–38.

West, E. (2022). *Culturally responsive classroom management for Native learners*. Indigenous Education Tools. https://indigenouseducationtools.org/bf/11

PART SEVEN

Cultivating Ubuntu Character

"A person with Ubuntu is open and available to others, affirming of others, does not feel threatened that others are able and good, for he or she has a proper self-assurance that comes from knowing that he or she belongs in a greater whole and is diminished when other are humiliated or diminished, when others are tortured or oppressed."
–Desmond Tutu

Ubuntu Character Development: Leadership

TEACHERS ARE LEADERS! A teacher is a leader that must lead from within. Teacher leaders have control of themselves and know how to navigate the space in which they collaborate with others effectively. The core values of teacher leaders are that they must have integrity, responsibility, and great pride in themselves.

A teacher is the class community's chief executive operator (CEO). As a CEO, the teacher's role comes with great power and responsibility. They must make sure that all the members are safe and secure. They understand that the class's success depends on their ability to help others see value in themselves and work as a team. As the class leader, it is incumbent upon the teacher to constantly work on building authentic relationships with the students and get students to work together in their learning space. Getting students to work together requires that the teacher operates from a problem-solving mindset. A teacher with a problem-solution mindset thinks of a potential problem or barrier to learning and seeks a solution. The teacher's goal is to activate or help draw knowledge from within.

A teacher's role and responsibility is to love and care for all the children. The teacher must supervise and manage all aspects of teaching and learning. The teacher's job is to motivate and shape a child's mind; however, it is not a good practice to use fear to get children to comply. Fear-mongering does not build autonomous and self-directed learners. Educators have used the whip and fear to govern students in my schools for many years, but those are not the best practices to support and guide learners. We also now know that when children are hurting, they hurt others. Fear as a means of discipline does not develop students who think critically and reflect honestly about their behavior.

Fear can be the easiest way to encourage or discourage a particular behavior, but that path is dangerous. Corporal punishment dehumanizes the child and creates added trauma. Instead, it is better to discipline a child with love to earn respect. When children learn to respect themselves and others, it promotes a harmonious learning environment. Children learn to develop into self-directed learners who take responsibility for their actions.

When students err, those situations should be used as opportunities to teach them. It is the teacher's duty to firmly correct students and provide opportunities for them to reflect, respond, and rehearse the desired behavior. The students should be held accountable for their actions, but embarrassing, chastising, and whipping them in front of the class are not the best practices.

When teachers are intentional and proactive about teaching, practicing, and reteaching the desirable behaviors, it fosters lasting bonds. In addition, it gives students the tools to manage their emotions and choices for a lifetime.

Cultivating an Ubuntu Discipline Plan

The term "discipline" is derived from the Latin word *disciplina*, which means to teach. Thus, the term "discipline" may be thought of as any training intended to develop moral character or produce a pattern of behavior. Good discipline must be cultivated; it does not come about by chance. It needs to be purposefully managed. Teachers must be proactive by setting high expectations, creating positive and safe learning environments, and providing students with the tools to resolve conflict (Nelsen,2006).

What Is Ubuntu Discipline?

Ubuntu discipline is a proactive humanistic approach that uses rituals, rules, and procedures to cultivate a positive mindset that will help to build a strong sense of responsibility in the community. Ubuntu discipline aims to help one develop themselves to work together for the common good in the community. In addition, a disciplined mind helps to create order in an ecosystem. Discipline is the ability to use rules and procedures to develop a sense of self-control and the practice of order.

In African axiology, when they say a person has Ubuntu, they are compassionate, caring, kind, and respectful. It is evident in the attitude and action of the person. When a person has Ubuntu consciousness, they affirm and dignify others. They create a hospitable environment for others to coexist. They deeply understand that one does not exist by oneself; we are interdependent. Ubuntu is the essence of being human. In an African worldview, a person is not solely defined by physical and psychological prosperities. However, a person is interconnected and interdependent upon the community. In African tradition, the self is the root of community. Individuals are taught that a person becomes a person through others, emphasizing interdependence. This understanding fosters harmony and balance within the community.

What Are Rituals?

Rituals are the daily actions to build the mind, body, and spirit. The purpose of a ritual is to strengthen our mental capacity. Rituals are what we do daily to bring meaning to ourselves and deepen our connections with each other. For example, meditating, doing yoga, martial arts, painting, journaling, singing, listening to music, and reading and writing affirmations are all forms of ritualistic behaviors. For centuries, rituals have developed deep connections to self and others. As a people, we are interconnected and interdependent; we are not humans by ourselves; we coexist with each other. The success of our community is a direct result of how we treat each other.

Cultivating Good Character

The discipline of a child starts in the womb of the mother. The mother is the first teacher, and it comes with great responsibility. When the child is in the womb, the mother should share positive stories and music with the unborn child. It is the first preparation for them to come into the physical world. The discipline of the mind should be an ongoing learning process from birth to young adulthood.

Parents and teachers must not spoil children. *Mwalumi* Baurti, a *jegna* and author of the book *To Educate A People* (2019), stated that a spoiled child would eventually become an adult with a negative, regressive character. A spoiled child often becomes an unmannered, selfish, and self-centered adult. Therefore, the educator must cultivate a disciplined child. Anyone who participates and invests in the child's growth and development is considered an educator. That could be the babysitter, grandparents, aunts, uncles, sports coach, dance teacher, and community members.

At each stage of a child's development, the parent and the child's teachers must teach the child how to control thoughts and actions.

From birth to age 3, a child learns how to govern emotions and listen to voices of command. Creating a routine for the child helps them develop order patterns in the brain. Set routines are a young child's first introduction to the discipline of the mind.

From ages 4 to 7 is a critical stage of a child's development. At this age, a child learns to trust self and the world. As the young child develops and learns more about themself and their place in the world, the parent must ensure more structure, rules, and procedures. Rules and procedures should be designed within the family and at school to help children understand boundaries. In addition to the rules and procedures, a child must be taught good manners. For example, teaching the child to use pleasantries such as "please" and "thank you" helps promote good manners. Good manners are one of the fundamental principles of a disciplined mind, and good manners play a significant role in building human relationships. Teaching manners helps the child understand the importance of respecting others and self.

Furthermore, educators must introduce children to character development concepts such as kindness, love, respect, honesty, caring, responsibility, and trustworthiness between ages 3 and 7. Cultivating a disciplined mindset in a child requires that the adults in charge explicitly teach the child good manners.

Young people must be taught moral values from ages 8 to 12. Teaching children how to love themselves and respect elders and others is crucial at this age. Family cultural values should be explained, and children should affirm them daily. For example, moral values such as MAAT principles should be introduced and reinforced. The seven principles of MAAT are Truth, Justice, Balance, Order, Harmony, Righteousness, and Reciprocity. Children must be taught how to use these moral values to govern one's daily lives. Children must be taught how to apply these principles. Parents and teachers can use songs, stories, role-play, and affirmations to teach young people how to develop a strong moral character. Additionally, the children must learn about the Ten Cardinal Virtues:

(I) control of thoughts
(II) control of actions
(III) have devotion of purpose
(IV) have faith in the ability of his master to teach him the truth
(V) have faith in himself to assimilate the truth
(VI) have faith in himself to wield the truth
(VII) be free from resentment under the experience of persecution
(VIII) be free from resentment under the experience of wrong
(IX) cultivate the ability to distinguish between right and wrong, and
(X) cultivate the ability to distinguish between the real and the unreal.

Educators must incorporate moral values into the family or the school's curricula to cultivate self-directed and well-mannered children. These values should be visible and reinforced daily.

From 13 to 18, the routines must be revisited and reinforced. If the child were exposed to a solid foundation of daily rituals and routines, their mannerisms and overall character would be evident. If the child makes errors, they should be used as a lesson to restore order and balance within the child. Around the age of 13, during puberty, it is a great time to introduce boys and girls to rites of passage. A rite of passage is a ritual, event, or experience that marks a significant milestone or change in a person's life. The rite of passage aims to strengthen the person's mental capacity and remind them that the family and community support them in new roles and responsibilities.

Adinkra Symbols and Teaching

What is the purpose of symbols, and how can they be used in teaching?

Research has shown that engaging students in the learning process increases their attention and focus, motivates them to practice higher-level critical thinking skills, and promotes meaningful learning experiences. Written symbols and signs have been integral to African systems of initiation and education for thousands of years. Symbols are the direct expression of thought. Ott (1989) stated that "symbols are signs that communicate meanings greater than themselves and express much more than their intrinsic content. They are invested with specific subjective meanings. Symbols embody and represent wider patterns of meaning and cause people to associate conscious or unconscious ideas that in turn endow them with their deeper, fuller, and often emotion-evoking meaning" (p. 21). Symbols are a powerful way to build relationships, connect students to information, and teach character development. However, symbols can also be used as instructional and engagement strategies. Engagement strategies are a variety of techniques educators use to help keep students' attention, curiosity, interest, optimism, and passion in the learning process.

Therefore, I use Adinkra symbols to enhance student engagement, maintain focus, and deepen understanding. As an instructional strategy, teachers can employ these symbols as a call-and-response technique and a motivational tool to keep students interested in the content. According to Willis (1998) in the Adinkra Dictionary, Adinkra symbols are meaningful icons from the Akan culture in West Africa. For instance, I use the *Pempamsie* symbol (see Appendix B) to signal students that I am about to teach something very important. The teacher says or shows the adinkra symbol: "*Pempamsie*!"
Students' response – *"I am a ready to learn!"*

The *Matie Masie* (see Appendix) symbol is used to remind the students that the information covered in the lesson is important and they should not forget it.

The teacher says or shows the symbol: *"Mate Masie."*

Students' response – "*What I hear, I keep*!"

Adinkra symbols such as Aya and Wawa Aba (Symbols D and E) can help promote a growth mindset and build resilience. When students develop a growth mindset, it motivates them to push through difficult situations. Teachers must explicitly teach students the symbols before using them as engaging strategies. Teaching adinkra symbols is a proactive approach to strengthening the students' character and the school's culture.

Reflection Questions

1. How do you conceptualize Ubuntu in your personal and professional life?
2. How can you integrate the Ubuntu Pedagogy Framework into your teaching practices?

References

Baruti, M. B. (2019). *To educate a people: Thoughts from the center*. Akoben House.

Nelsen, J. (2006). *Positive Discipline*. Ballantine Books.

Ott, J. S. (1989). *The organizational culture perspective*. Dorsey Press.

Willis, W. B. (1998). *The Adinkra dictionary: A visual primer on the language of Adinkra*. Pyramid Complex.

Appendix A

Adinkra Symbols

SYMBOL A: Dicipline

Akoko Nan[1]
Discipline With Love
Affirmation:
I am love.

Akoko Nan is an Adinkra symbol that looks like a hen's foot. The symbol shows how nurturing is intertwined with discipline. In the Akan culture, they have a proverb that says, "*Akoko nan tia ba na enkum ba,*" which means "The foot of a hen steps on the (chick), but it doesn't kill the chick." The proverb reminds us that discipline must be tempered with love, mercy, and patience. Discipline methods should be humanizing instead of dehumanizing! Teach children what is expected of them. When they err, use it as an opportunity to teach them to correct the behavior. Remind them about the importance of obedience.

One way to get the point across to young children is to share stories and folktales. For example, in Ghana they have an aphorism that says "An obedient child is a happy child! A disobedient child is a sad child!" This is an excellent aphorism to remind children about the importance of doing what is right without someone watching them.

SYMBOL B: Knowledge

Mate Masie
Affirmation:
What I hear I keep.

Mate Masie is an Akan Symbol of wisdom, knowledge, and prudence. The implied meaning of *"mate masie"* is "I understand." Understanding means wisdom and knowledge, but it also represents the prudence of considering what another person has said. The symbol is used to help learners remember the information they are taught.

SYMBOL C: Readiness

Pempamsie
Sew in Readiness
Affirmation:
I am ready to learn.

Pempamsie is an Akan symbol of readiness, steadfastness, and hardiness. The symbol resembles the links of a chain and implies strength through unity and the importance of being prepared. This symbol is used in teaching to draw the learners' attention to crucial information we want them to remember.

SYMBOL D: Perseverance

Wawa Aba
Affirmation:
I will not give up.

Wawa Aba symbolizes hardness, strength, toughness, and perseverance. This symbol encourages us to persist even in challenging times.

Motivational song lyrics are a powerful way to build resilience. In a world often filled with challenges, it's important to remind children that we can collectively find the strength to overcome difficulties. The version of the song "Something Inside So Strong" by South African singer Lira reminds us to push through difficult times:

"The higher you build your barriers the taller I become the farther you take

my rights away the faster I will run You can deny me You can decide to turn your face away No matter because there's... Something inside so strong I know that I can make it."

Teachers can incorporate songs with motivational messages to encourage students even when things are difficult.

SYMBOL E: Endurance

Aya
Affirmation:
I am a winner.

The ***Aya*** symbol represents endurance and resourcefulness. The symbol represents the fern plant because the plant adapts well to different environments and is very durable. Educators can use the *Aya* (fern) symbol to encourage students to focus on their goals. Teachers must teach students how to set goals and remind them to stay focused on their goals while looking at each step along the way. In addition, educators can use the ***Aya*** to promote a growth mindset. A growth mindset is a way of viewing challenges and setbacks. People who have a growth mindset believe that even if they struggle with specific skills, their abilities aren't set in stone. They see failure as an opportunity to grow. When children develop a growth mindset, they acknowledge and go through fears rather than around them and often discover new strengths within themselves.

SYMBOL F: Kindness

BI NKA BI
Kindness, Peace, and Harmony
Affirmation:
I am kind.

The adinkra symbol, ***BI NKA BI***, means "*No one should bite the other,*" or peace and harmony. This symbol warns us against cheating, lying, backbiting, and the provocation of others. It encourages children to play fairly and be cordial with each other.

SYMBOL G: Cooperation

Boa me na me mmoa wo
"Help me and let me help you"
Affirmation:
I am helpful.

The adinkra ***Boa me na me mmoa wo*** symbolizes cooperation and interdependence. It reminds us to work together and contribute positively to the community because strength lies in unity. "Help me, and I will help you." This symbol is a great way to promote unity among children.

SYMBOL H: Leadership

Adinkrahene
Affirmation:
I am a leader.

The ***Adinkrahene*** is a symbol of leadership. It reminds us that leadership comes with great responsibility. Educators can use this symbol to teach children about leadership. Teach students those great leaders that have integrity. This symbol exemplifies the honorable qualities of a good leader. A good leader must love and care for themselves. Good leaders must have respect for themselves and the people.

SYMBOL I: Learning from the Past

Sankofa
Affirmation:
I am a learner.

The word SANKOFA is derived from
SAN (return)
KO (go)
FA (see, look, take)
The word Sankofa means that we should learn from our past. This symbol has many applications; however, teachers can use it to help students feel confident about relearning information they have not mastered yet.

Why Proverbs Are Important

Proverbs are excellent tools for building students' morals and values. They contain deep wisdom and cultural insights, helping to tell stories and activate prior knowledge. Proverbs are based on real-life experiences and are passed down from generation to generation, teaching important life lessons. Using proverbs in the classroom can enrich students' understanding of their culture and help them develop strong ethical values.

List of Proverbs and Aphorisms

- "An out-of-control adult cannot do anything to help out-of-control young people."
- "I am because we are."
- "When teachers lose control, no one wins!"
- "Beware of your own feelings and thoughts. It is important in helping to navigate difficult situations."
- "A man of character is a man of wealth."
- "If you want to go fast, go alone. If you want to go far, go together."
- "If you have no confidence in self, you are twice defeated in the race of life. With confidence, you have won before you have started." –Marcus Garvey
- "Ubuntu teaches us that we are all bound together in ways that can be invisible to the eye; that there is a oneness to humanity; that we achieve ourselves by sharing ourselves with others and caring for those around us." –Barack Obama

"Know Thy Self"[2]

"A person who knows not and knows not that they know not is foolish—disregard them. A person who knows not and knows that they know not is simple—teach them. A person who knows not and believes that they know is dangerous—avoid them. A person who knows and knows not that they know is asleep—awaken them. A person who knows and knows that they know is wise—follow them. All of these persons reside in you. Know Thy Self and to Maat be true."

–Anthony T. Browder

A modern adaptation of an ancient proverb

[1] Adinkra.org

[2] (From "Nile Valley Contributions to Civilization, Exploding The Myth, Vol. 1" by Anthony T. Browder)

APPENDIX B

Cultural Identity

Know Thy Self: Who Am I

Before developing cultural knowledge and awareness about others, we must uncover and examine personal social and cultural identities. This guided self-reflection allows us to understand better how our identities inform who we are.

Identify at least four facets of self:

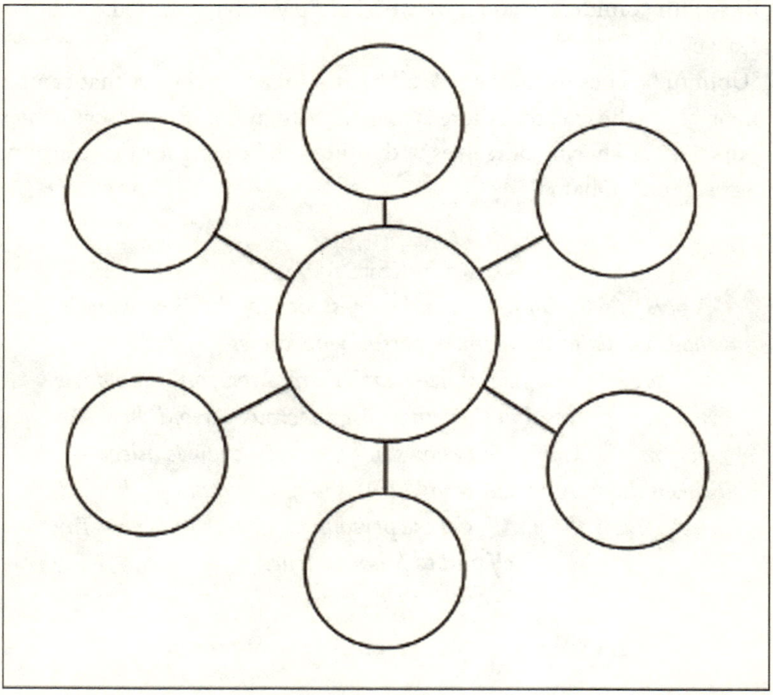

APPENDIX C

How Is Ubuntu Expressed in Other Countries?

Countries	***How Ubuntu is expressed in other cultures***
Angola	*Gimuntu*
Azania (South Africa)	*Ubuntu/Botho*
Botswana	*Botho*
Burkina Faso	*Maaya*
Burundi	*Ubuntu*
Cameroon	*Bato*
Congo Democratic Republic	*Bomoto/bantu*
Equitorial Guinea	*Maaya*
Gambia	*Maaya*
Ghana	*Biako ye*
Kemet (Egypt)	*MAAT*
Kenya	*Utu/munto/mondo*
Liberia	*Maaya*
Malawi	*Umunthu*
Mali	*Maaya/hadama de ya*
Mozambique	*Vumuntu*
Namibia	*Omundu*
Nigeria	*Mutunchi/Iwa/Agwa*
Rwanda	*Bantu*
Tanzania	Utu/Obuntu/Bumuntu
Uganda	*Obuntu*
Zambia	*Umunthu/Ubuntu*
Zimbabwe	*Hunhu/Unhu/Botho/Ubuntu*

Countries in Diaspora	***How Ubuntu is expressed in other cultures***
United States of America	*Kwanzaa:Nguzo Saba (African-American)*
Brazil	*Iwa*
Haiti	*lakou*
Jamaica	I n I (Rasta language =Iyaric)

APPENDIX D

Comparative Analysis of Ubuntu Pedagogy and Traditional Pedagogy

Aspect	Ubuntu Pedagogy	Traditional Pedagogy
Philosophical Foundation	Rooted in the African philosophy of Ubuntu, emphasizing the interconnectedness of humanity, compassion, dignity, and collective solidarity (Ukpokodu, 2016)	Grounded in Western individualistic and Eurocentric worldviews (Ukpokodu, 2016; Dei, 1996)
Learner-Teacher Relationship	A partnership of co-creators of knowledge promotes mutual respect, care, and affirmation of our shared humanity (Letseka, 2012)	Traditional pedagogy often has a more hierarchical power dynamic (Ukpokodu, 2016)
Classroom Environment	Democratic, where students feel respected, cared for, and empowered to co-learn (Blackwood, 2018)	Can be more authoritarian in nature (Ukpokodu, 2016; Freire, 1970)
Learning Process	Cooperative learning, drawing on diverse perspectives and experiences to build knowledge collectively (Venter, 2004)	It tends to be more individualistic and competitive (Ukpokodu, 2016)
Cultural Affirmation	Affirms students' cultural identities and Indigenous knowledge as valuable assets (Blackwood, 2018; Letseka, 2012)	Has often marginalized non-Western cultures and knowledge systems (Gay 2010)

Goals	Cultivates social values like solidarity, cooperation, and human dignity alongside academic learning (Ukpokodu, 2016)	Primarily, it focuses on mastery of academic content (Apple, 2004)
Cultural Restoration	Seeks to restore the cultural identities and values of students that were eroded by colonial education systems and hidden curriculum (Ngubane & Makua, 2022)	Has historically been a tool for cultural assimilation (Dei, 1996)

About the Author

Alecia Blackwood, an experienced and passionate master teacher with over 20 years in education, is not only an author and international speaker but also a former Fulbright-Hays Scholar for Namibia and Botswana. Throughout her career, she has shared her knowledge worldwide and served as an education consultant for various institutions, including private and Catholic schools, public schools, nonprofit organizations, and homeschooling families across Canada, America, the Caribbean, and several African countries. Dr. Blackwood is recognized as one of the leading experts in the United States on Ubuntu pedagogy, a humanistic approach to fostering student engagement in teaching and learning. In addition to her scholarly pursuits, she actively volunteers with a nonprofit organization that provides cultural education for Black students. Furthermore, she leads the Sankofa Youth Initiative, a study abroad program that offers middle and high school students the opportunity to engage in STEAM projects in Ethiopia and Ghana during the summer. In 2024, she was awarded a fellowship by the International Society of Technology Education (ISTE) as a faculty research fellow, where she is engaged in research on artificial intelligence in school environments. Currently, Dr. Blackwood is an Assistant Professor of Education at Longwood University, where she passionately mentors aspiring educators and instills innovative teaching methods. Beyond her academic commitments, Alecia enjoys embarking on travel adventures, indulging in gourmet cooking, cherishing precious moments with her family, and doing yoga.

Index